HOLY WAYS OF THE CROSS;
OR,
A SHORT TREATISE ON
THE VARIOUS TRIALS AND AFFLICTIONS,
INTERIOR AND EXTERIOR,
TO WHICH THE SPIRITUAL LIFE IS SUBJECT,

And the means of making a good use thereof.

TRANSLATED FROM THE FRENCH
OF
HENRI-MARIE BOUDON,
ARCHDEACON OF EVREUX.
BY EDWARD HEALY THOMPSON, M.A.

Dicebat autem ad omnes: Si quis vult post me, abneget semet-
ipsum, et tollat crucem suam quotidie, et sequatur Me.—
Luke. 9:23.

LONDON:
BURNS, OATES, & CO., PORTMAN STREET
AND PATERNOSTER ROW.
1875

1

ISBN: 978-0-9769118-7-6

Printed and Bound in the United States of America

Published by:

St Athanasius Press
133 Slazing Rd
 Potosi, WI 53820
1-608-763-4097
melwaller@gmail.com
http://www.stathanasiuspress.com

Email is the best way to reach us.

Check out our other titles at the end of the book!

Specializing in reprinting Catholic Classics!

ADVERTISEMENT.

To those who are acquainted with this admirable little book, redolent as it is throughout of that sweet perfume of piety which so peculiarly distinguishes the works of the saintly writer, no special reasons need be assigned for giving it an early place among these "Select Translations for Spiritual Reading." But, if any were needed, one might be found in the present crisis of the Church's fortunes, when all the powers of the world and of hell seem to have combined together, with a might and a determination which men destitute of faith may deem to be irresistible, to crucify the Son of God afresh and put Him to open shame in the persons of His holiest members, and especially of him whom He has constituted the visible head of His mystical body. " If one member suffer anything, all the members suffer with it," says the great Apostle (1 Cor. 12:26): how much more when it is the head itself which is the victim of wrong and violence! Amid the present darkness and distress this little book may help to minister consolation and inspire drooping hearts with courage, by reminding them that suffering is the Church's heritage, the very condition of her well-being, nay, her highest privilege, inasmuch as it renders her most like to her Divine Spouse and is the pledge and surety of her triumphs. As of the Lord Himself (Luke 24:26), so of His Church it may be truly said that she ought to suffer these things and so to enter into her glory. Her most signal successes have been preceded, and indeed attended, by humiliations and apparent failures, and have been accomplished, like all the great designs of God, under the heavy weight of the Cross.

Perhaps, too, the chapter in which the venerable author, with that power of vivid realization which is so remarkable in him, describes the reasoning with which moderate minded and, apparently, God-fearing people among the Jews discussed the question as to the guilt or innocence of Jesus, and contrived to remain insensible to the awful iniquity which their rulers were perpetrating in crucifying the Lord of Glory, may help to explain to perplexed observers at the present day how prejudice, interest, human respect, repugnance to sanctity, and a general hatred of the supernatural so blind the eyes and pervert the judgments even of those who, to all appearance, are men of sterling probity and sincere religious feeling that they are able to ignore, excuse, and even to approve and justify, or, at least, to view, not only without moral indignation, but with complacent indifference, the outrages to which Christian men and Christian women are being subjected, in violation of every principle both of natural justice and of public law, and to regard their sufferings as the result of their own wrong doing, their imprudence and intemperance, or their short-sighted adherence to exploded ideas and obstinate resistance to the spirit of the times—in other words, to the evil ways and false maxims of a world whose friendship is the enemy of God.

And here it may be observed how earnestly this holy man insists, with St. Paul (2 Cor. 10:5), on the necessity of " bringing the understanding into captivity" to faith, and rendering a sincere and entire submission to the decisions of Sovereign Pontiffs, no less than of General Councils, because, as successors of St. Peter, they have received an express commission from Christ to confirm their brethren: thus confounding those who perversely dream that the doctrine of Papal infallibility is a novelty in the Church. " O blessed they," he proceeds, " who, obeying in simplicity the Pope and the Church, have remained faithful to their religion! The Lutherans and Calvinists of the last century"— and his words are as applicable to the innovators and blind leaders of our own day—" cried out that the Pope was in error, and that they desired a General Council: but afterwards, seeing themselves condemned also by the Council, they said that it was not a legitimate one, on account of the Pope's intrigues and, in saying these things, they awfully deceived themselves, together with all their adherents, whom they involved with themselves in everlasting damnation. Those who were living at that time, and who adhered to Sovereign Pontiffs and to Councils, preserved the faith for themselves and their posterity; and if we live in a Catholic country we owe it to their obedience." And so also—it may be added—if the true religion has been preserved within this realm of England, it is due to the heroic constancy of our forefathers in the faith, and their undying devotion to the See of Peter. God grant that all we their descendants—some of us, indeed, born out of due time—may prove true to the precious inheritance which they have bequeathed to us!

It is not, however, of exterior trials and sufferings that the author principally treats, or of those obvious temptations to which all Christians are exposed, but of those deep interior miseries, those subtle devices of self-love, those illusions and preternatural assaults of the evil one, which, in some form or other, they must be prepared to encounter who strive to pursue the arduous paths of spiritual perfection. And if testimony were wanted to the high character and the great practical usefulness of the work, it might be sufficient to cite the words of the doctors in theology who were commissioned to examine and report upon its contents previous to its publication in the year 1671. From the terms in which their approbation is couched, it will be seen that the doctrine which the treatise enforces, as it is necessary for all times, so is particularly applicable to our own, when men who profess to represent the highest intellects of this boasted age of progress are inviting Christian people to exchange the truths of divine faith and the life-giving lessons of the Cross for the base, uncertain tenets of a sensual philosophy and of a false and godless science.

" It is a book," say they, " as full of instruction for souls which desire to rise to perfection as for those whose office it is to direct them on their way. We have found in it a teaching all divine, which the light of faith alone is capable of rendering intelligible to those who read it, and which divine love alone can enable them to relish. It is a knowledge which God hides from worldlings who allow themselves to be guided by their senses, and from men of mundane policy who regulate their actions by the sole light of human reason. This science of the Cross, unhappily, is ignored, neglected, or despised by the greater part of men, comprising even a number of the learned, who, devoting all their life to the study of the speculative sciences, pay no regard to the science and the maxims of Jesus Crucified, ' in whom' nevertheless ' are hid all the treasures of wisdom and knowledge' (Col. 2:3). It may be hoped," they add, " that the reading of this book will inspire those who peruse it with the desire of dying wholly to themselves and following Jesus Christ, seeing that it is replete with the unction of the Spirit of God."

The whole treatise, in short, may be taken as an exposition in detail, by an accomplished master of the spiritual life, of that comprehensive chapter in " The Following of Christ," which bears the title " Of the King's Highway of the Holy Cross."
E. H. T.
Cheltenham,
Feast of St. Peter and St. Paul, 1875.

CONTENTS.

PART I.

The Science of the Cross.

CHAPTER I. 25

THE SCIENCE OF THE CROSS IS A HIDDEN MYSTERY.

This mystery was hidden from Jews and Gentiles; and even from Christ's own disciples. It is unintelligible to the wise of this world; however great their learning. It is opposed to worldly pride and delicate living. Many professedly devout persons ignorant of it. To be learnt only by Christian simplicity and mortification

CHAPTER II. 29

WHETHER IT BE PRUDENT TO WRITE RESPECTING THE WAYS OF THE CROSS.

A counter opinion stated. This opinion opposed to the practice of the doctors and masters of the spiritual life. The Lives of the Saints abound in relations of interior trials. The ill use made of such reading no argument against the treatment of the subject. The knowledge of it necessary in many cases. The valuable instruction thereby afforded. The compassion due to souls so terribly afflicted

THE WAY OF THE CROSS IS THE ROYAL HIGH ROAD TO A BLESSED ETERNITY.

It is the road by which all Saints have passed. Examples from Holy Scripture. Security of those who walk therein. The ways of consolation full of peril: by-paths at best, from which it is easy to go astray. The way of the Cross is rough but safe

WE MUST OF NECESSITY WALK IN THE WAY OF THE CROSS.

Crosses are inevitable on the way to Heaven. Sin must be punished. As the Head suffered, so must the members. Our Lord preached the doctrine of the Cross openly and to all; and pressed it-on His disciples. To be a Christian and to be crucified one and the same thing

THE HAPPINESS OF A CHRISTIAN CONSISTS IN SUFFERING IN THIS WORLD. REPLY TO CERTAIN OBJECTIONS.

Several reasons given for this assertion. In particular, the grace of Jesus is a crucifying grace. Most crosses sent to those whom God loves most. Testimonies to the blessedness of suffering from Scripture and revelations made to Saints. Suffering necessary to draw man out of his state of corruption. Life a state of warfare, and therefore of suffering. Crosses necessary for perfecting the soul. They endure throughout life, and, if withdrawn for a while, are given back. Crosses are profitable, and even necessary, in order— 1. To satisfy the Divine Justice; 2. To purge the soul of its imperfections; 3. To humble us; 4. To increase our grace and merit; 5. To bring us into closer conformity to Christ. How God refreshes His elect. The joy that is promised and enjoined not a sensible joy; but that which resides in the superior region of the soul. Abuses and faults may occur in the holiest states, but do not detract from the perfection of those states. The dangers of spiritual consolations. Jesus the true pattern of the elect; His refusal of joys and satisfactions. Ought, then, guilty man to be exempt from suffering? The value of suffering taught by Christ's example. The true import of His teaching. Testimonies thereto from Scripture and maxims of Saints

CROSSES ARE A MARK OF PREDESTINATION, AND OF A HIGH PREDESTINATION.

The thought of Eternity; how little pondered. Suffering the portion of the elect. Express testimonies of Scripture to this truth. It is a law which knows no exception. The greatest Saints have borne the heaviest crosses. Sufferings serve to the increase of eternal glory

CROSSES EXALT TO MATCHLESS GLORY.

No glory to be compared with that of the Cross.

Remarkable language of St. John Chrysostom and St.
Augustine. Our Lord's own words, and those of St. Paul.
The suffering and the indigent exhorted to recognize the
exceeding privileges of their state

CROSSES ARE THE EARTHLY PARADISE.

No Paradise without God; crosses unite to God. This union
the source of solid happiness. Often more perfect the less it
is felt and known. No rest save in God alone. Happy effect
of meditating on crosses

PART II.

Exterior Trials.

THE WAYS OF THE CROSS ARE VARIOUS

All true Christians walk by the way of the Cross; but not
all alike. Great variety of sufferings; the creature bound to
submit to the Creator's behests. Our Lord's whole life one
continued suffering

EVERYONE MUST BEAR HIS OWN CROSS, AND IN
THE MANNER GOD WILLS.

All who belonged to Christ have borne their cross. Three

things of which we must beware:—1. Not to procure ourselves crosses by our own faults; 2. Not to occupy ourselves with desiring other crosses than those we have; 3. Not to delude ourselves with desiring to bear our cross in a different way from that which God appoints. We must turn our crosses to the best account. To which end we must look simply to the will of God

CHAPTER III. 77

WE MUST BEAR OUR CROSSES IN THE MANNER GOD WILLS.

The soul must blindly follow God's will, and not make reflections on itself. Disquietude of mind a stratagem of the devil. Sensible repugnance to suffering no proof of unwillingness to suffer. Impossible to escape temptations by our own efforts. Self-abandonment necessary in order to attain to perfect indifference. God never refuses His aid. In the strength of Jesus we shall be able to endure and to overcome. We must not relax in our spiritual exercises although we feel nothing but repugnance to them

CHAPTER IV. 82

CORPORAL INFIRMITIES.

Bodily defects a favor of Heaven. Bodily ailments a great grace, which must be utilized for Eternity. Pretexts of self-love. Incalculable blessings obtained by suffering souls. God, who wills infirmities, wills also the inconveniences and afflictions which they entail. Persons of very great virtue often so sensitive to pain as to be constrained to cry aloud from their excessive sufferings

for the more perfect abasement of the elect. The use made thereof by the devil

ABANDONMENT BY CREATURES AND PARTICULARLY BY FRIENDS.

The being forsaken by friends a grievous affliction; but in losing friends the true Christian finds God. No one so utterly forsaken as Jesus. The thought of this excites a holy desire of being abandoned by all; the vastness of the subject. Blessed exchange: God instead of creatures. Interior abandonments most profitable

PART III.

Interior Trials.

OF INTERIOR SUFFERINGS; AND FIRST OF TEMPTATIONS TO UNBELIEF AND BLASPHEMY.

These sufferings far surpass all exterior sufferings. Temptations against faith most terrible. Many Saints have endured them; examples. We must not argue with such temptations; danger of so doing. Heresies come from the exercise of private judgment; duty of sincere submission to the Pope and the Church. The remedy against such temptations lies in avoiding all voluntary reflections. Acts of faith real, though unconscious; proofs of this.

Temptations to blasphemy frighten more than they hurt; resistance mistaken for consent. The Lord Himself thus tempted. Sentiments of St. Teresa on this subject

CHAPTER II. 112

TEMPTATIONS TO DREAD OF REPROBATION, DESPONDENCY, AND DESPAIR.

Many holy souls have been thus afflicted. God desires our salvation more than we do ourselves; proof in the Incarnation, Crucifixion, and Blessed Eucharist. The remedy is to abandon ourselves to Divine Providence; an heroic act of love. Our God Infinite Goodness. Frequent falls no ground of discouragement. These interior sufferings the chastisement of sin: this of itself a motive for courage. Temptation a sign of election; the devil assails those who are the true servants of God

CHAPTER III. 117

OF DRYNESS, DARKNESS, DISTRACTIONS, AND REPUGNANCE TO PIOUS EXERCISES.

Instances of holy persons who have been tried by spiritual dryness. How St. Catherine of Genoa suffered from interior darkness. Saints not exempt from painful distractions; striking confessions of St. Jerome and others. States in which the soul becomes devoid of feeling. That which renders us pleasing to God is, not feeling or the want of feeling, but the free action of the will. Remarkable instance in the person of Father Jognes. How we ought to deal with distractions. Consoling thoughts under such affliction.

CHAPTER IV. 123

OF TEMPTATIONS AGAINST PURITY.

Exciting causes of such temptations. They may be made the occasions of great victories and great rewards. This consideration a consolation to souls so afflicted. Such trials contribute much to spiritual advancement; examples from the Lives of Saints. Chastity does not consist in insensibility but in resistance. Remedies recommended.

CHAPTER V. 127

OF DOUBTS AND SCRUPLES.

No temptations can sully the soul so long as they are displeasing to it; the doubt whether we have consented itself a mark of not having consented. Origin and occasions of scruples. Need of a charitable and enlightened director. St. Ignatius most severely tried. Persons so afflicted ought not to repeat their confessions. Neither ought they to confess their temptations or sins about which they have a doubt; they ought to avoid long examinations of conscience, and abide by the judgment of their director. Submission of spirit absolutely necessary; subtle inventions of self-love. We must combat 'our scruples with courage; instances of peace of mind being restored by simple obedience.

CHAPTER VI. 136

OF SUFFERINGS CAUSED BY THE DEVIL.

Instances of ordinary temptations. Persons of extraordinary virtue tempted by the devils in an extraordinary way. These eminent souls the special objects of their malice. Their efforts to deter persons from practicing mental prayer, and especially the highest order of prayer. Instances of exterior diabolical assaults. Their interior assaults most formidable. The craft and subtlety of these spirits of hell. Remedies against these temptations, ordinary and extraordinary. Directors of souls so terribly tried ought to be men of great enlightenment. In cases of possession, the exercise of the will not free; although the sufferers maybe obstinate in declaring that they consent with full deliberation. This state most humiliating, but one of the most effectual for attaining a high degree of sanctity. The devil flees before resolute souls. He has no power to force the will. Holy Communion the most effectual defense against his attacks. His efforts to prevent persona from communicating.

CHAPTER VII. 150

OF SUPERNATURAL SUFFERINGS.

These come immediately from God, and are most terrible. Father Simon de Bourg's description of such trials: the soul deprived, not only of reflective acts, but of the power of making many direct acts. St. Teresa's more detailed account of these suffering states. Similar reflections of another spiritual writer. Mysterious dealings of God with certain souls. Case of an innocent soul afflicted with all the effects and emotions of sin. "The exile of the heart": these words of " The Following of Christ" very little understood.

CHAPTER VIII. 156

THE SAME SUBJECT CONTINUED.

These extraordinary sufferings inflicted by God in order to perfect the soul in virtue and defeat the artifices of self-love. Divine annihilations; none comparable to that of Jesus. These crosses reserved for God's dearest friends. Signs which distinguish a passive state of suffering. What a soul so afflicted must do. The immense advantage of these interior pains.

Prayer To Our Lady Of Martyrs 163

PART IV.

The Value of Crosses.

CHAPTER I. 164

OF THE CAUSES OF CROSSES.

Crosses are sent to punish us for our sins. To purge us of our faults, and especially our secret faults. To sanctify our souls. In fine, we suffer because we are members of Jesus Crucified.

CHAPTER II. 167

WHY GOD OFTEN DOES NOT HEARKEN TO US WHEN WE PRAY HIM TO DELIVER US FROM OUR SUFFERINGS.

All crosses come from God, and God is Sovereign Reason; they are therefore always just. They are also always profitable, however painful. Dereliction of our Blessed Lord upon the Cross; revelations to Saints

17

THE PERFECT CROSS, AS EXEMPLIFIED IN THE PERSON OF THE SERAPHIC ST. TERESA.

Few crosses are completed. St. Teresa a prodigy of grace. The vastness of her cross; constructed of such a variety of materials. Her body one whole cross. Her own testimony to this. The sufferings of her soul intense, beyond description. The divine favours she received afforded her no consolation. The saint's own description of her torments; for which she found no relief. The opposition she encountered almost universal. She is rebuked by her confessors, threatened by magistrates, insulted by the populace, upbraided by her own friends, denounced by prelates, condemned by doctors. The slanders, ridicule, and ill-treatment to which she was subjected. She is falsely accused before the superiors of her Order, and the authorities of the Inquisition; her own General forsakes her. Her exalted virtues declared to be fictitious. The reasoning of human prudence. How they are refuted and stultified by Almighty Wisdom; example of the Patriarch Joseph. St. Teresa sorely tried by evil spirits. Sufferings the means by which the saints are made partakers of Christ's glory

Prayer To The Most Holy Virgin, The Crowning Perfection Of God's Works 212

TO OUR LADY OF PITY.

Holy Virgin,---this little work comes to lay itself at Your sacred feet, like all the others which have proceeded from my hands, as a thing that belongs to You in my quality of Your slave; and, because You are my sovereign mistress and august queen, I venture to dedicate it to You, relying on Your unimaginable goodness, as Lady of all Pity, Your sorrow never having had its like among pure creatures: and, in truth, if sorrow has love for its foundation, it must fain be said that Your has never had its equal, since Your love can suffer no comparison. Thus are You ever incomparable, in whatever way we may regard thee. Justly should all creatures melt into tears, and all hearts be torn with anguish, at the contemplation of Your dolors; but for myself, I ought to live no longer after beholding a spectacle so sad and piteous. I declare to You, O my holy princess, that I ought to have long since died of grief at the thought of Your exceeding sufferings; and yet I do avow that I am utterly unworthy of so great a grace. Deign at least, O most pious and most sweet Lady, to receive with Your accustomed benignity this little work, dedicated to God Alone in Your honour, as a mark of the respect which I wish to render to Your sorrows, and a testimony both of the great compassion which I feel for them and of the love which I desire to show them for the remainder of my life. Oh, from the very depth of my heart, from the inmost recesses of my soul, I would that every line and every word of which it is composed were so many voices to cry aloud, from earth to heaven, that I desire to have all possible share in all Your sorrows as well a in all Your joys, in all that has afflicted as well as in all that has consoled thee! I would wish they were as many tongues to bless and render everlasting praises to the Most Adorable Trinity, for the inflexible firmness and invincible courage wherewith You were endowed amidst all the storms and tempests by which Your blessed heart was assailed, but never shaken. Permit, O glorious Lady, this poor heart of mine to give vent to these effusions of its love in Your amiable presence, and obtain for me, and for those who shall read this book, some share in Your love and fidelity to the holy ways of the Cross. Amen.

TO ST. JOHN THE EVANGELIST AND THE BLESSED MARIES ON CALVARY.

Blessed Saints of Calvary, a thousand times more blessed in the ignominy of that place than if the Almighty had set you upon thrones the most august on earth, having prostrated myself at the feet of our common sovereign, the worthy mistress of this mount of love and of the Cross, I come to throw myself at your feet also, there to offer you this work, which breathes only of the interests of God Alone in the holy ways of His sufferings.

Amiable Saint, beloved of Jesus and of Mary, next to our incomparable Mother this little book belongs to You, by a thousand titles of obligations inconceivable, which I owe to Your loving goodness; but it belongs also to You as being the great disciple of the Cross, as well as of love, seeing that our Divine King paid You the exceeding high honour — -be astonished, O ye Seraphim!—of causing You to drink of the cup which His Eternal Father had given Him, and made You a man of sorrows after the likeness of Himself. Therefore was He pleased to make You a faithful witness of the consummation of His sufferings on the Cross, and that, in this state of crucifixion, all Christians should be exalted, in Your amiable person, to the glorious privilege of children of His most holy Mother, who travailed in birth of us to God amidst that boundless sea of sorrow with which her virginal heart was inundated at the foot of the Cross. No wonder, then, that You should speak so willingly of sufferings; as You did make plainly evident to St. Elizabeth of Hungary, when, appearing to her in sensible form, whom Heaven had by a special privilege placed under Your particular direction, the sole favour You did promise her was that crosses should not fail her.

And You blessed lover of the Son of God, glorious St.

Magdalen, I come next to offer this little treatise to You, as to her who kept watch with unshaken fidelity by the Cross of our good Master. Many waters of affliction and of contradiction were powerless to quench the ardors of Your noble heart, all burning with love for the Adorable Crucified, whom You did love so fervently as even to ravish with delight the sublimest intelligences of Heaven, those spirits of purest love. And truly, at the sight of this, justice demands that the hearts of all the faithful should love thee. O great Saint, my heart desires to pay the debt of love it owes You, at least according to the measure of my poor ability; in Your charity, then, be pleased to accept this little testimony of its love which it here presents thee.

O blessed Mary, mother of James, and thou, too, Salome, I offer to you also this work of the Cross with most respectful reverence and all the affections of my heart. Many reasons oblige me thereto, but especially the very ancient and immemorial devotion of the diocese of Evreux to your holy persons, which celebrates your festival on the 23rd October throughout its whole extent, and makes it a solemnity of the first class in its cathedral church, and that, too, with no common honours; having, moreover, in this church a chapel specially dedicated to your glory, whither the faithful come to pay their devotions and offer their adorations to the Most Adorable Trinity, which- in Its great mercy and goodness, has exalted you to this great glory together with the extraordinary privileges wherewith you are endowed. And yet farther, many fair churches, consecrated to God under the invocation of your holy names throughout my own archdeaconry, are also to me very pressing motives for rendering you some testimony of my respect. But the alliance which Heaven has accorded you with Mary, Mother of Jesus, and, consequently, with Jesus, Son of Mary, and, above all, the constant, faithful love which you displayed towards this God-Man Crucified, irresistibly constrain me to manifest the high esteem which I have conceived of your eminent sanctity, and the ardent desire with which I am possessed that it should be better known and loved. Ah! Would that I were able to make known everywhere your admirable perfections; would that I were able to make them loved by so many who know them so little, and are so little affected by them! Yes, O great Saints, were it only in my power, devotion to you should be the practice, not of the diocese of Evreux alone, but of every diocese in the land! O my Lord and my God, increase it more and more in places where it is established, and bestow it on those which have it not. Make me worthy, according to the multitude of Your great mercies, to contribute somewhat thereto, by Your aid, in this diocese of Evreux, and especially through the archdeaconry which I hold, and hold purely by an extraordinary favour of Your holy Mother, into whose hands I have committed it, and now again do entirely commit it under the patronage of the glorious St. Taurinus, first apostle and patron of the diocese—and by a particular Providence, I write this on the 11th day of August, the feast of that holy bishop—that he may dispose of it without reserve according to Your good pleasure.

O You faithful lover, and you, O faithful lovers, of Calvary, receive, then, this slight testimony of my love and reverence, and obtain for me the benediction of the Adorable Jesus Crucified and of His Virgin Mother, and for those also who shall read this little treatise for the honour and glory of the Cross of our Saviour, who lives and reigns with the Father and the Holy Ghost forever and ever.

PART I.

THE SCIENCE OF THE CROSS.

CHAPTER I.

THE SCIENCE OF THE CROSS IS A HIDDEN MYSTERY.

There can be no manner of doubt that the science of the Cross is a hidden mystery, seeing that the Divine Word teaches us so. It is that hidden mystery of which the Apostle speaks to the Ephesians (3:9); and which he tells us, writing to the people of Corinth (1 Cor. 1:23), was "unto the Jews a stumbling-block, and unto the Gentiles foolishness." Strange, that this mystery, the great master-piece of the wisdom of a God, should have passed for a folly among the nations, and that the ablest minds, the finest intellects in the world, should have made a mock of it! In such wise it is that the human mind, shut up in itself and using only its own lights, apprehends divine things. Ponder thereon, ye who read these lines, and learn from the feebleness of the light of the human intellect to value only the splendors of faith. But what is still more astounding is to see that the Jews understood not this mystery, although it was accomplished before their eyes, and they had in their hands the Scriptures and the prophecies which had foretold it in so many places. Nay more; when the Incarnate Wisdom revealed it to His disciples, even to them it was still a hidden word: they had no perception of it—they even feared to have any further knowledge of it. The Son of God disclosed the secret to them, but it remained none the less hidden from their eyes through lack of disposition; so that when their Divine Master spoke to them of the humiliations of this profound mystery, the Gospel tells us (Mark 9:33) that their thoughts were occupied with a point of honour, and at that very time they were desirous of knowing which of them would be the greatest. O my God, to be so near the light, and an infinite light, yet not to see! How was it possible not to learn under such a master? Oh, what a subject of humiliation, or, rather, of annihilation, to a creature! After this, let us cease wondering if every day we still see so many Christians, the disciples of this same Master, ignorant of this mystery, although they make profession of honouring it: the reason is, that they are far removed from that spirit of mortification and self-annihilation which disposes the soul for the understanding of this divine secret.

This wisdom of the Gospel is not understood by the wise of this world, whose wisdom is death, according to the testimony of the great Apostle, who expressly declares (Rom. 8:6, 7) that it is " an enemy to God; for it is not subject to the law of God, neither can it be,"—words which, duly pondered, ought to inspire a great fear, a horrible dread, of that accursed " wisdom of the flesh," which is nothing but folly in the eyes of God and of the holy angels. Ye great intellects, ye bright geniuses, who are so much esteemed and admired by the creatures of earth, learn now that all your wisdom is veritable foolishness; learn, O men, the estimation in which you ought to hold them, and try, by the help of grace, to extricate yourselves from the illusion of the world, whose judgment is utterly opposed and directly contrary to that of God. Oh, what misery, and the source of miseries which will never end! To despise what God esteems, to esteem what God despises: such is the maxim of the wise of this world! Is it not for this that the great Apostle cries (1 Cor. 3:18), "Let no man deceive himself: if any man among you seem to be wise, let him become a fool " 1 To be wise in the eyes of God, a man

26

must be like one demented in the eyes of the world, whose
thoughts are mere vanity, whose wisdom is condemned
of God. Let us say, then, with the same Apostle (5:21), "
Let no man glory in men": in their sentiments, which are
nothing but illusion; in their esteem, which is nothing but
deception; in their judgment of things, which is nothing
but error. Their state being so deplorable, how should they
understand the hidden mystery of the Cross 1 No; men of
the world will never understand aught about it, however
many books they may read, and however many sermons
they may hear.

The proud and self-sufficient will never understand it, for it
is written (James 4:6) that God resists them and departs far
from them. Alas! If they who approached nearest to Light
Itself, the Incarnate Wisdom, understood it not before the
coming of the Holy Spirit, how shall they understand it
who are immersed in darkness 1 In vain may they pursue
studies long and deep, take degrees in the schools of
philosophy and theology, make themselves proficient in the
highest sciences, and be even teachers of them, —if all this
be accompanied with pride and self-sufficiency, these men
will still be ignorant of the science of the Cross; and, with
all their learning, they will never succeed in mastering its
A, B, C. They will be utterly incapacitated for the study of
this science, and altogether disqualified for admission into
its school.

The desire of honour is in formal opposition to the
knowledge of this mystery, which imparts not itself to
those who place their joy in the esteem and applause of
men, and in the friendship of creatures, while they dread
their contradictions and rebuffs. Lovers of themselves, who
labour to minister gratification to their mind and body, and
who seek- only themselves, shall have no understanding of

it. The ignominies and humiliations of the Cross are very hard to be discerned amid the blaze of worldly honours. How is it possible to have any knowledge of its pains, or any taste of its sufferings, amid the comforts of life? Soft clothing and soft beds, sumptuous furniture, luxurious living, are so many thick veils which hide from us the sight of the Cross. Alas! What connection has the vain and deceitful delicateness of a worldly life with the hardness of that saving Wood? The Emperor Heraclius, desiring to carry the Holy Cross on which the Son of God had been crucified, was unable to move a step so long as he remained arrayed in his royal robes; to enjoy this honour he was obliged to put on poor and humble clothing. 1

(1 On recovering the True Cross, which had been carried into Persia fourteen years before, the Emperor Heraclius brought it back to Jerusalem, and would have borne it on his own shoulders, in solemn procession, up the Hill of Calvary, but found himself withheld, as by some invisible power, from passing out of the city gates. Then, at the suggestion of the Patriarch, who reminded him how little the pride and pomp of his apparel accorded with the ignominious appearance of the Son of God when He went forth bearing His Cross, he laid aside his crown and purple, and, putting on mean clothing, was able to accomplish his pious purpose.)

But that which is most deplorable is to see so many persons who make profession of devotion, who talk of it, who preach it, and yet are very little instructed in the knowledge of this mystery. The great secret for having a true enlightenment respecting it is practice: that is, a practical experience of poverty, pain, contempt, contradiction, desertion, repulse, ignominy; and, as this experience is more commonly the lot of simple people, whose life is one of suffering, and the privation of what the world esteems, it often happens that poor simpletons and weak ignorant women are deeply versed in this doctrine, while the learned have no knowledge of it whatsoever. Thus, O Eternal Father, has it seemed good to You to order: " You have hid these things from the wise and prudent, and have revealed them to little ones" (Matt. 11:25). Let us take good heed, then, to walk always in Christian simplicity; and, to use the Apostle's comparison, in his second Epistle to the Corinthians (11:3), let us fear lest our minds should be corrupted, as Eve was seduced by the subtlety of the serpent. " Take heed how you hear," says the Scripture (Luke 8:18). Ah, how difficult it is, never hearing honours, pleasures, and the goods of this life mentioned except in terms of the highest esteem, not to allow ourselves to be corrupted by the sentiments of the world, through adopting its maxims.

CHAPTER II.

WHETHER IT BE PRUDENT TO WRITE RESPECTING THE WAYS OF THE CROSS.

The question here proposed is not whether it be fitting to speak or to write in general of the ways of the Cross; for it is sufficient to be a Christian to know that it is, not only fitting, but even necessary to speak, think, and think again and again, of the ways by which all the disciples of the Son of God must needs walk. The difficulty is as to whether it be good to treat in particular of certain interior crucifying ways, on account of the consequences which may ensue from doing so.

There are persons who say that these pains ought not to be written about, because the imagination of the weak-minded is easily impressed by the description they read of them; they figure to themselves imaginary states of that kind, and fancy they are walking in very exalted ways; thus scandalizing others and bringing contempt upon themselves. Yet the practice of the directors and masters of the spiritual life is altogether opposed to the opinion of these persons. The books which they have published leave no room to doubt the truth of this. If I were called upon to particularize, I should have to cite almost all the great writers who have treated of the mystical ways. I will content myself with quoting what St. Bonaventure has written on the subject. That holy doctor, treating of the interior crucifying ways, says that first there comes a withdrawal of devotion, then a weariness of praying, hearing of good things, speaking of them, or doing them, and of assisting at divine offices. Next, a person is tempted to be impatient with God, even to the extent of asking himself why God is so- hard: and this temptation is so violent that it puts a man almost beside himself. But (proceeds the Saint) the sorest trials are temptations to falter in the faith, to despair of the mercy of God, to blaspheme against God and His Saints, to live in a certain perplexity of conscience, full of alarms and complaining, and at last to be deaf to all salutary counsel. So far I have given the words of this holy doctor. I say nothing of St. Jerome and St. Bernard, who believed they were glorifying God by bequeathing to posterity a knowledge of the temptations which they suffered against purity, and of which they specified many particular circumstances. Neither do I speak of the great Apostle, who desired that the whole Church should know of his sufferings in this respect (2 Cor. 12:7). It is impossible that he could have lacked discretion in leaving them on record, seeing that he was guided by the Holy Spirit in writing as he did.

We cannot justly impute blame to the Fathers of the Church who have treated of these interior pains, for certainly they were not wanting in light, prudence, charity, and experience. Even those holy women and blessed virgins who have given their writings to the world have treated of these ways of suffering: as, for instance, among many others, St. Catherine of Genoa and the Blessed Angela di Foligno, whose extreme sufferings inspire the deepest feelings of compassion, as St. Francis de Sales has averred. And has not St. Teresa spoken of interior pains in many passages of her writings? The reader will have occasion to observe how strong are the testimonies which we shall adduce in the present work in very many places. The authors of the Lives of the Saints have felt no difficulty in relating all their sentiments and sufferings. We need only peruse the lives of persons eminent for their sanctity, as well those who lived in the first ages of the Church and throughout all subsequent times, as those also who have appeared in our own days. Do we not read how a St. Benedict threw himself into a bed of thorns from the violence of a temptation against purity; and how a St. Francis cast himself down in the snow under the pressure of a similar trial? St. Peter Celestine, again, suffered grievous agonies from the same temptation. There were some who were afflicted during their whole life. The history of St. Francis de Sales shows what distress he endured on the subject of his salvation; while that of the Mother St Jane Frances de Chantal lets us see what extreme sufferings she underwent during the whole course of her life. The history of St. Ignatius tells us of the torments he suffered from scruples, to such a degree that, that great Saint was tempted to despair. The life of the St Mary Magdalen of Pazzi exhibits interior crosses which were terrible. In fine, the writings of the Fathers of the spiritual life and the histories of Saints are filled with ways of suffering.

If, then, it was not fitting to write of them, we must condemn the Fathers of the Church, suppress the books of the mystical doctors, and banish from us the whole history of the lives of Saints. But, it is said, many make ill use of them. I reply that directors ought to be careful not to permit the souls they are guiding to read books which are not profitable to them, and that every one ought to beware of using what affords him no aid, or proves an obstacle, to his advancing in the path of perfection; and therefore we ought to choose such works as are suitable to us, and not make use of all sorts of spiritual books indiscriminately. And if it happens that some do not make a good use of them, we must not therefore condemn the books on account of such abuse: otherwise we must blame the Holy Scriptures, which so many heretics have abused, and the writings of the Fathers of the Church, and, in fine, whatever is most sacred in religion.

But why write about these matters? The holy doctors have done so, and that alone is sufficient to convince a reasonable mind that it is both useful and necessary to write and to speak of them. But further, we may say that it is needful to treat of these things for the sake of a number of persons who are walking in these ways of suffering, and who, living in small towns and country villages, are without any one who is capable of furnishing them with light concerning these states. One must have passed along these painful ways in order to know to what misery the poor soul that undergoes them is reduced. In the midst of all these grievous pains, what is to become of her, knowing not what to do, often tempted to despair, and imagining herself to be already lost; and, what is still worse, finding confessors so little enlightened as to take her temptations for sins, and help her only to bewilder herself in a manner that is incredible to such as have no experience of these kinds of torments and sufferings? If we seriously consider the character of these pains, which surpass everything which it is possible to suffer exteriorly, and their consequences, which reach even to Eternity, and the great want of assistance which is the usual lot of those who are so sadly situated, we shall come to agree that these persons stand in urgent need of succor. A poor man dying of hunger is in a condition which creates the strictest obligation to relieve him; but the state of which we are speaking carries with it something far more pressing. It is no question of the life of the body, which must be lost sooner or later: it is question of the salvation of a soul, which is of infinite moment. Now the light which is imparted by books which treat of interior crosses to the persons who are so afflicted, instructs them as to the value of such states, and the love and tenderness of Divine Providence which sends them, although It may seem to be treating them with great severity; it teaches them how they ought to comport themselves, fortifies and encourages them, sustains them amidst their dejections and temptations, their despondency and despair; and enables them to profit by their trials or by the chastisements with which the Divine love and justice is pleased to visit them. Many confessors and directors who are not sufficiently experienced in these ways receive abundant light by the reading of these treatises; and, to crown all, the Adorable Jesus is thereby greatly glorified in His members, who are never more closely united to Him than when they are most conformed to Him in His crosses. The charity of Jesus Christ, therefore, constrains me to put forth this little work, for the promotion of His glory, and that of His most holy Mother, in crucified souls.

Even the little experience I have myself had makes me see most clearly that these souls are supremely deserving of compassion, and that of all suffering persons they are the most afflicted. Let such as make but small account of their crosses pardon me, but it is not possible for me to doubt that these crosses are terrible. Let them pardon me such modicum of zeal as it pleases our Lord and the Blessed Virgin to give me in their behalf. When one is penetrated, however so little, with a sense of the length of Eternity, the torments of Hell, the bliss of Paradise, and, above all, with the exceeding charity—I repeat it, the exceeding charity— of a God-Man, dying on a gibbet, amid an intensity of suffering which the human mind cannot comprehend, for the succor of souls, it is not possible to pass so lightly over their needs: nay, what is there that one ought not to do? O Adorable Heart of Jesus, open to us; O Furnace of Love, show Yourself to Your creatures; O Ineffable Charity, O Exceeding Mercy, make Yourself known. It is to You, it is for You, I write this book; bless it, and draw from it Your own glory, and that of most holy Mary.

CHAPTER III.

THE WAY OF THE CROSS IS THE ROYAL HIGHROAD TO A BLESSED ETERNITY.

There are many ways, O my God, which conduct to Your blissful joys; there are many paths which lead to Your glorious Eternity. But, O my God, You have made a highroad which conducts thereto with the surest certainty. Now, my soul, this highroad is none other than the way of the holy Cross. This way is the royal highroad of all the elect, for it leads to the royal city of the King of kings. It is the royal highroad; for it is along this way that the great company of the Saints advances, together with the Queen of Saints and the great King of Paradise. It is the royal highroad of salvation; for it is by it that the messengers of a blessed Eternity carry the sweet dispatches of grace; it is by it that the great convoys of needful provisions go; it is by it that all the precious merchandise of beauteous Paradise is conveyed. Let us remount, O my soul, to the very beginning of the world, and thence descend from age to age to our own latter days; let us consider with attention all that has passed under the law of nature, the written law, and the law of grace; and we shall most clearly see that the way of the Cross has ever been the royal highroad of the elect.

If I behold an Abel who is pleasing to God, I see at the same time a Cain who persecutes him. An Abraham must be subjected to the last ordeal by the command he receives of sacrificing his only son. Job shall be reduced to a dunghill, to a state of extreme dereliction; despised by his friends, mocked by his own wife, and despoiled of his goods and of his children. Moses has a Pharaoh to try him; David, an Absalom, his own son; Elias, a Jezabel; Tobias- loses his sight, and is in danger of losing his life. St. John Baptist has a Herod, who will put him to death. All the Apostles and disciples are men of the Cross. If innocent babes are among the throng, the feebleness of their age will not exempt even them from this road of suffering; for, because they belong especially to God, they will be all bathed in their own blood, their life will pay the forfeit, that life which they have but only just received. In a word, the Church sings, "What great torments all the Saints have suffered!" In fine, O my soul, see how the King of Saints, He who is the Way, the Life, and the Model of all the souls that shall be saved, walks with giant steps, or, to speak more truly, runs along this road, from the first instant of His Divine Conception to the last moment of His life. Consider how the most holy Virgin, His blessed Mother, bears Him company; and St. John the Evangelist, His beloved disciple, St. Mary Magdalen, His faithful lover, and, to say everything in few words, all those whom He has most favored with His love. Remember how the Scripture teaches us (Apoc. 7:14) that those who have been pleasing to God have passed through many tribulations, and have been made His friends by the trials He has sent them.

Great security, then, for all who tread this road, seeing that it is the royal highroad of salvation: he who walks therein proceeds in full assurance. O soul, whoever You are, why do You disquiet Yourself in this way of the Cross? I think I hear those blessed ones, who know so well the roads that surely lead to a glorious Eternity, cry aloud to You, " Fear not, it is well with thee; You walks securely; You are treading the royal highroad to Heaven. From thieves and murderers You have naught to dread, for they flee before the Cross with more swiftness and affright than do men before the artillery of earth or the lightning of heaven."

It is not so in the ways of consolation, temporal or spiritual; there our invisible foes gain easy access, secrete themselves, and lie concealed; there the flesh gathers strength, nature renews its life, self- love finds aliment, and the spirit of the world creeps in.

These pleasurable ways, albeit spiritual ways, are very dangerous, for it is very easy to deceive ourselves in them. Although we are able to go to God by them, and may go to Him by them, we are often greatly surprised at finding ourselves, unwittingly, walking in the path of nature instead of in the way of grace. The sensible sweetness which proceed from grace, the consolations which come from the satisfactions we receive in this life, satisfactions innocent in themselves, are little byways which may lead to Heaven but these little paths go across country; at times we have a difficulty in tracing them, occasionally they fail us altogether, and we do not know where we are. We are being continually embarrassed by the thousand divergences they oblige us to make. Often we have to knock at doors and ask the road, in order to ascertain whether we have not lost our way; and we must give unwearied attention, or we shall be sure to go astray. But in the royal highroad of the Cross we have only to walk on and follow the path: a blind man might keep to it without losing his way, guided by the sound of those who are proceeding along it. It is altogether needless to ask for directions: everyone who is well instructed in the matter will reply, "You have only to take care and walk straight on; you cannot go wrong, unless you deliberately choose to quit this highroad of the Cross, in order to follow the ways of consolation and satisfaction."

For the rest, you must not be troubled if this road wear an ugly appearance: it is true there are many rivers to wade through, but the bottom is sound; you may walk steadily on; there is nothing to fear. He who should choose to turn aside, that he may walk more at ease among meadows covered with flowers, where all looks smiling, would not go far without meeting with ditches which he would be unable to cross, or without plunging suddenly into some morass, from which he would not be able to emerge except with great difficulty. The safest course is to keep to the highroad trodden by all the Saints of Paradise. There is no danger in walking along the road of the Son of God and His most holy Mother. O my Saviour, I see Your footsteps imprinted on this road, most clearly do I perceive Your traces; draw us after You, and never permit us to go astray in the ways of the world. We ask You for this grace and mercy by Your exceeding love and charity, by the most loving heart of Your dear Mother, and by all Your Angels and Saints. Oh, how deplorable is the blindness of the world, which seeks none but easy paths! But how great is the happiness of those who bear their cross, following in the steps of an Incarnate God and His Virgin Mother!

CHAPTER IV.

WE MUST OF NECESSITY WALK IN THE WAY OF THE CROSS.

We cannot question what the Divine Word asserts: consequently we must believe the way of the Cross to be necessary, for this is what it teaches us. Follow as many paths as you please, in which you have a taste of innocent pleasures—if they lead to Heaven, the roses that grow therein will always have their thorns. Granted that hard and heavy crosses form the royal highroad of Paradise, crosses of small or moderate size will always be found in all the ways which may lead thereto; for it is a dictum pronounced by the Holy Spirit Himself (Acts 14:21): "that through many tribulations we must enter into the Kingdom of God." Observe: the Holy Spirit does not teach us that it is becoming, or that it is useful, or that it is better to suffer; but it says distinctly " we must." Suffer, then, we must: we have no choice in the matter.

In truth, the quality of sinner in itself calls for sufferings; for God, who is most just, cannot leave crime unpunished: His justice chastises it either in this life or in the other. But as beatitude is reserved for His servants in the other life, it is therefore necessary that their faults should be punished in this world; and, on the other hand, with the exception of the Virgin Ever Immaculate, even in the first instant of her most Holy conception, all men have sinned: therefore all men ought to bear crosses.

Nay, the very quality of Christian does not permit our

being exempt from sufferings; for, if it was necessary that the Adorable Jesus, the Head of all the faithful, who make with Him one only mystical body, should suffer, and so enter into glory, as the Divine Word assures us (Luke 24:26), much more ought the members to be afflicted. In the natural body, if the head or the heart be in pain, all the other members suffer with it. No one is at ease when these principal parts are in suffering. But who could imagine that the king should enter into his kingdom, which belongs to him of right, only by dint of wounds, and that the slave of devils, who deserves hell, should possess it without it costing him anything? " Keep well in mind those words of Scripture," said our gracious Saviour to St. Teresa: " ' The servant is not greater than his lord'" (John 13:16). This is a palpable truth; but, alas! Why do we not apply it to ourselves? " Where I am," our Master likewise said, " there also shall My servant be" (John 12:26). Most just; and how act otherwise, seeing that we have also the very great honour, the inconceivable honour, of being His members? How shall the Head go one way and the members another? You who read this must see clearly that it is impossible,— unless the members separate themselves from their Head: in which case they will be members without life, dead and rotten members, no longer fit for anything but to be cast into the fires of Hell. Let us say, then, as we meditate on this truth, Alas! Of what are we thinking, when we think not to suffer? It is to desire the impossible; and that is the greatest folly in the world. Oh! With what exceeding justice does our Master cry out in St. Luke (14:27), "Whosoever does not carry his cross, and come after Me, cannot be My disciple." Weigh well these words: " cannot be." He does not say, " he will hardly be," but " he cannot be."

Such, then, is the great doctrine of the Cross, which our Lord preached to all the people. He did not disclose to them all the mysteries of the Kingdom of God; and although He gave the knowledge of these to His disciples, as He Himself testifies (Luke 8:10), there were nevertheless many things, as He declares (John 16:12), which He did not say to them, because they were not yet able to bear them. But as to the doctrine of the Cross, He proclaimed it openly, without any reserve and without any delay, O human prudence, what becomes of You now? Does it not seem that it would have been well to wait until this gross-hearted people,' to whom our Good Saviour spoke, was better disposed? If this Divine Master reserved certain things to be said, even to His disciples, till after the coming of the Holy Spirit, was there anything apparently which ought more to have been thus reserved than a doctrine so severe, and at that time almost unheard of; and that too when it was question of a people altogether carnal? And all the more because this people, instead of profiting by it, were scandalized and murmured at it—to such a degree that some among them wanted to cast down a precipice this Divine Master who taught it, and His kinsmen sought to lay hold on Him and bind Him, declaring He was a madman (Luke 4:29; Mark 3:21). Why preach a doctrine which produces such effects? Yet He spoke of it publicly and openly; and to all He said (Matt. 16:24), "If any man will come after Me, let him take up his cross." He said it to all, to His disciples and to the carnal minded multitude; and He spoke of it so indiscriminately as to make no exception. " If any man will come after Me,"—that is to say, whoever you be, rich or poor, learned or ignorant, high or low; be you general, prince, king, or emperor; whatever be your rank and condition, or age, whether young or old, man or woman; whatever be your state, whether living in the world or retired from the world,—if any one among you will come after Me, let him take up his cross: he must make up his mind to suffer. This is why the Gospel tells us (Luke 9:44) that when His miracles were noised abroad and filled those who beheld them with wonder and amazement, He diverted His disciples from the thought of them, and bade them lay up in their hearts the words He had spoken to them of His Death and Passion, of which He discoursed to them at the time of His most miraculous acts, in order to teach them that it was not consolations on which our minds ought to be fixed in this life, but rather on toils and sufferings.

1 Matt. 13:15.

What are you saying, then, O Christian, when you complain of your sufferings? Reflect seriously on the title you bear. To be a Christian and to be crucified is one and the same thing. If you renounce suffering, you must renounce Christianity. I ask you once again—Do you really know what it is you are doing when you talk of not suffering? Do you wish to give up the Christian religion, deny your baptism, and cease to be the disciple of Jesus Christ? Now, if you wish to remain so, prepare yourself for suffering, either of mind or body; either from the contradictions of men, which are never wanting; or on the part of Hell, which will fight against you; or from your own corrupt nature, your inclinations, your passions, your humors. Bear well in mind what the Church sings;. "Hail, O Cross, our only hope." There is no hope but by this way.

CHAPTER V.

THE HAPPINESS OF A CHRISTIAN CONSISTS IN SUFFERING IN THIS WORLD REPLY TO CERTAIN OBJECTIONS.

If the way of the Cross is necessary to salvation, what greater happiness can there be than to find ourselves in it?

And, on the contrary, is there any misery comparable to that of being out of it? But if it is the royal highroad, as has been shown, is it not a great happiness to be walking securely in it? This is why (as I shall notice hereafter) the Cross is the true mark of predestination; and, indeed, the members are saved by their conformity to their Head. Further, let me ask, is it not a signal blessing to be in a state of suffering, seeing that in the judgment of the Saints there is no glory to be compared with that which belongs to crosses? The way of the Cross is the great indubitable means which, by separating us from creatures, unites us to God; and is it not in this union that the good of goods, the sovereign good is found? O my soul, what a blessing sufferings are! They are (said a holy person) our fathers and our mothers, who have generated us on Calvary. They who will not receive them are like those who drive their father and mother from their house. St. Teresa declares that it is an illusion to think that our Lord receives any one whatever to His friendship without putting him to the test by sufferings; and her great director, the venerable Father Baltasar Alvarez, speaking on this subject, said, " If the Superior of a house were the first at prayer in the morning, and at the other exercises, and the rest remained in bed, without doubt he would be displeased; with far greater reason, then, would our Lord, being who He is, and having been first to take up the Cross, be dissatisfied at finding no one willing to bear Him company."

Let me repeat it: the happiness of sufferings is incalculable, because he who has the Cross has everything. It purifies and satisfies; it delivers and saves; it beautifies and adorns; it enriches and ennobles. It is profitable to the good and to the bad; for it causes the one to advance on the way to virtue, and it purifies the others from their faults, and procures pardon for them. Moreover, we must say, what cannot be too often repeated, that they who are saved, are saved only by the same grace which is in Jesus: otherwise the spirit of Jesus would be in contradiction to itself, and wholly different in the Head from what it was in the members. Now the grace of Jesus is a grace which nails and fastens to the Cross. The spirit of the Cross is the spirit of our spirit; it is the life of our life. They who suffer most, said a servant of God, fill up most that which is wanting of the Passion of the Son of God; for that which is wanting is the application of its fruit: the application of a grace which has its source in sufferings, is effected much better by crosses than in any other way.

St. Teresa declared that our Lord sent most crosses to those whom He most especially loved. She had learned this doctrine from the very mouth of the Son of God, who had said to her, " My Father sends the heaviest trials to those whom He loves most." It is sufficient to know the facts of our holy faith to be thoroughly persuaded of this truth. Never was any one more beloved by the Eternal Father than the Divine Jesus; and never did any one suffer so much-Next to Jesus, the most holy Virgin surpasses all creatures in graces, and at the same time she surpasses them in sufferings. The measure of our happiness must therefore be taken from the measure of our crosses. Happy he who suffers; more happy he who suffers much; most happy he who is weighed down with all sorts of sufferings, whose daily food is the Cross, who spends his whole life thereon, after the pattern of our gracious Saviour and His holy Mother, and at last thereon expires.

But further, it is a truth of faith that the happiness of this life consists in mourning: " Blessed are they that mourn," said Truth Itself (Matt. 5:5). Now by mourning is meant all those subjects of sorrow which may happen to us, and which are capable of touching us and moving us to tears; and our Divine Master, being pleased to explain somewhat more of these subjects in detail, assures His Apostles (Matt. 5:10, 11; Luke 6:22, 23), that they will be blessed when they are reviled, and all manner of evil is spoken against them untruly; when they are hated, rejected, driven out, and their reputation wholly ruined. This is why the Holy Spirit emphatically declares in Scripture (James 5:2), " Behold we account them blessed who have endured "; and He adduces the testimony of the Two Testaments, the Old Law and the New, that by the examples of Job and the Adorable Jesus all doubts that might be entertained upon this subject may be removed. Hence the great Apostle, instructing the faithful, teaches them (Phil. 1:29) that, besides the gift of faith, the gift of suffering has also been granted to them. And this deserves to be well and deeply considered, in order that we may esteem it as we ought: for, in fine, this gift of sufferings is a great gift of God. Thus the Blessed Virgin revealed to a holy person who endured pains the like of which are not to be found in all the lives of the Saints, that she had used all her influence to obtain them for her; and for the same end had caused her to undertake many toilsome pilgrimages, extraordinary fasts, and a number of other mortifications. It is related of this same holy person that, on praying to our Lord in behalf of a poor tradesman who was cruelly harassed by some soldiers quartered in his house, that good Saviour told her that the man in question was under great obligations to these soldiers: because they served as instruments of Divine Providence to make him suffer.

The human mind, however, impelled by a secret love of self, does not lack arguments to allege in opposition to this doctrine of the Cross. " What pleasure," it will urge, " can God take in these ways of suffering? What good does He

44

draw from them to souls, or what glory to His Holy Name? Surely God is in Himself all goodness; His pleasure is to do good, and to load His beloved creatures with good things. His purpose in creating man was, not to make him endure sufferings, but to make him lead a happy life in this world and the other." This is true, looking only at the primal state of things: but man, having become depraved and corrupted by sin, doomed himself to suffering; which is necessary in order to draw him out of his corruption, and re-establish him in a state of salvation. This is why God sends him sufferings, as a good father makes a sick child who is dear to him take bitter medicines. Ah! Surely he would be glad not to subject his child to this affliction; but his child is sick, and therefore he is constrained to do so: it is his very love which impels him to act thus. Hence it is easy to see the good which accrues to souls from sufferings, and the glory which the All-Good God derives from them; for their fruit is everlasting salvation. Oh, what happiness, what consummate happiness! This truth will be made abundantly plain in several subsequent chapters of this little work.

This is hard to understand, some one will say. Here, then, is what the great prelate De Belley says in answer to this difficulty in the sixteenth chapter of The Spiritual Conflict: "This will seem hard to believe," wrote this great man; " but if you remember that the rowers as they sit have their backs turned towards the place to which they are taking their boat, you will find nothing strange in that God should make you work your way to peace and refreshment by the fire and water of tribulation." And in the sixth chapter of the same book: " Who does not know that trees, the more they are shaken by the wind, the deeper do they strike their roots; that incense does not give out its sweetness until it is burned; that the vine bears little fruit unless it is pruned? Why so many scourges, so much poverty, so many pestilences, famines, wars, and other miseries, except for the good of the elect? Did not the Son of God place the consummation of our salvation in the consummation of His sufferings, and in His very dereliction by the Eternal Father?"

But sufferings, it will be replied, are not the end for which spiritual states are designed. Very true;. but they are the means which conduct thereto. Do you desire to make no use of them, on the pretext that they are only means? Rome is the destination which a man proposes to himself, when he designs to visit this first city of the world; all the cities, towns, and villages which lead thereto, are but intermediary stages through which he must pass: yet he must needs pass through them, or he will never arrive at his journey's end. Now, as long as we are in this life, we are still " in the way "; we shall not reach our end absolutely and entirely till after death; and in this world we have unceasingly to fight: which is not done without suffering. Hence it is that Scripture teaches us (Job 7:1) that the life of man upon earth is a battle or a warfare; and the Son of God gives His disciples, as their portion in this life, mourning and tears.

It will still be rejoined that even in this life states of suffering the most crucifying lead to the enjoyment of God. Granted: but this joy, as St. Augustine most truly teaches, is not experienced upon earth in its full perfection; and this is why it is not exempt from crosses, which in this world are always sent, in order either to purify the soul more and more, or to beautify, adorn, and enrich it more perfectly. From whatever side you view the matter, you will see the need of crosses, because there is always room for purifying or perfecting more and more. This is clear, so far as respects perfection, from the sufferings of the most holy Virgin. I allow that there are certain crucified states which

46

are only temporary, certain sufferings which are only for certain occasions, or for certain dispositions incident to peculiar interior states. God is the master; He knows how to apply them according to His sovereign wisdom; to some more, to others less. I allow that there are certain souls which, through divine grace, suffer with so much courage that they seem not to be suffering while they suffer. We shall show, in the course of the present work, that the ways of the Cross are various: nevertheless, they are all ways of the Cross.

All that we have to do in these divine ways by which we are led, is to be in them in such wise as God wills us to be. It is not for us to make crosses for ourselves: we have but to receive them from the hand of God, whether they be large or small, heavy or light, according as it shall please Him to dispose them. Only it is necessary to beware of an illusion into which some spiritual persons are betrayed, who, under the pretext of joy in God, would introduce us, even in this life, into a state which is all consolation and delight, and speak of sufferings as things which are only for a time. I admit, as I have already said, that there are certain crucifying ways which are not lasting; but this is not a general rule, as is evident from the example of many Saints, who have endured extraordinary interior pains during the whole course of their life. For instance, a St. Hugh, who was thus tormented to the very hour of his death; and in our own times, that holy man, Father John of Jesus-Maria, General of the Discalced Carmelites, who testified, when dying, that he was not even then free from these pains; as also the Venerable Mother de Chantal, who appears not to have been delivered from them even in her last mortal illness.

There are those whom God conducts by a mixed way of

sufferings and consolations; which made a servant of God express himself as follows:—" As the goldsmith from time to time draws his work out of the fire, manipulates it, and examines it to see if it is wrought into shape, and, not being perfectly finished off, thrusts it back into the furnace; in like manner God sometimes withdraws a soul from afflictions, and gives it consolations, but, being still not thoroughly purified, it is cast back into its sufferings."

God is always infinitely adorable and amiable in His dealings. He is the Sovereign Master, who does well all that He does. It is not for human nature to scrutinize them; its duty is to resign itself to them blindly, with complete submission and perfect love. Ever most true it is that crosses are good for us, in whatever state we may be:

First, to satisfy the Divine Justice, in union with the satisfactions of our good Saviour. Alas! We have deserved to suffer forever in Hell for our sins; we have deserved to be deprived of the Presence of God, and of all consolation, for all eternity: have we any reason, then, to be surprised if we have to endure pains and privations during the whole course of a life which so soon passes away?
Secondly, we have always need of being purged of our imperfections. We have said it already: there is always something in us to be purified during this life; Saints are liable to imperfections, and it is certain that the least imperfection hinders our entrance into Heaven. Hence it is, as we are told, that some holy souls, admirable for their virtues, which have even passed through interior states of extreme suffering, have had nevertheless to go to Purgatory. " Our whole life," said St. Francis de Sales, " is but a novitiate; we shall not make our profession, our complete and entire profession, till after death."

Thirdly, crosses are necessary in order to humble us. This is the opinion of St. Gregory, who teaches that he who is rapt highest in contemplation is most harassed with temptations. The example of St. Paul is an incontestable proof of this truth. This is the reason, according to the doctrine of the same Father, why we often experience the greatest pain from the very thing which we had set up as our resting-place. Hence the Prophet has truly said (Ps. 40:4), " You have turned all his bed in his sickness ": as if he had said, " All whatsoever a man had prepared for his repose, You have changed into trouble to him."

Fourthly, crosses are always profitable because they serve to the increase of grace, of the love of God, of merit, and of glory. Wherefore it is that our Lord has allotted so large a portion of them to those souls regarding which He has great designs. " Thus it is," says St. Teresa, " that He has dealt with His Saints: loading them with sufferings, after having imparted to them His graces and a sublime gift of prayer." It is related of the holy Mother de Chantal that our Saviour recompensed her sufferings with fresh afflictions.

Fifthly, the conformity of the members with their Head requires their being crucified with Him—with Him who was never for one moment without suffering, and who, at the very time that He communicated of His glory to His Sacred Body on Thabor, had it present to His mind, and discoursed concerning His dolorous Passion. The glorious St. Ignatius, founder of the Company of Jesus, penetrated with this truth, declared that, in cases where equal glory would accrue to God either from consolation or from suffering, he should always prefer suffering, because it brings us into closer similitude to our Divine Master. " Oh, what a shameful thing it is," cried St. Bernard, " to see a member given to delicacy under a Head crowned with thorns!"

Here it may be objected that our Saviour says (Matt. 11:28), " Come to Me, all you that labour, and are burdened, and I will refresh you." Now certain it is that God, who is faithful to His promises, will refresh all His disciples: but how? He will refresh them by the everlasting rest which He will give them in the other life; He will refresh them in the present life by the strength He will give them to bear their crosses; and this is common to all who suffer:
for, though the strength He gives be not equal in all, the grace He bestows is abundant in all crucified souls. He will refresh them at times by sensible consolations; but this is not the lot of all. He will refresh them also by delivering them from particular pains; but this, it must be observed, is not to be understood as implying, ordinarily, either a sensible alleviation or an entire deliverance from these afflictions: for how could such a doctrine be reconciled with the notorious condition of so many holy souls, which have appealed to Jesus Christ for succor, and nevertheless have continued in their state of suffering?

We shall still be met with those words of the Apostle (Phil. 4:4): " Rejoice in the Lord always "; whence it will be concluded that happiness consists in rejoicing. But this objection is easily answered: for the Apostle means either a sensible joy, or a joy which resides in the supreme region of the soul, and which is very often imperceptible. Now, to say that he means a sensible joy is quite impossible: for it would be going against all experience, against everything we read in the Lives of Saints, against all the teaching of the Fathers of the Church and of the masters of the spiritual life, and against the authority of Scripture itself in the mouth of this same Apostle, whom we should make guilty of a manifest contradiction; seeing he declares (2 Cor. 1:8) that he himself was "pressed out of measure," and not only exteriorly, but that his interior anguish was such that at times life was a burden to him; and this, not only from the longing desire he had to see Jesus Christ, but also from the greatness of his tribulations, which made him say that he was " weary even of life." It is plain, therefore, that this constant rejoicing of which he speaks cannot be understood of sensible joy, for in this world of ours such joy is not lasting. He speaks, then, of a joy which resides in the superior region of the soul], and comes from that abundance of peace which is the result of perfect conformity with the Divine Will; for the soul, willing only what God wills, is always content whatever may befall it.

Now, this peace, or this joy, is often so hidden that not only have the senses no share in it, but not even the inferior reasonable portion of the soul. I have treated at large, in my book, On the Reign of God in Mental Prayer, of the difference between the inferior reasonable faculty and the superior portion of the soul: a difference which it is very necessary to note, for many even learned men confound the two, and understand by the inferior part the sensitive and animal. The example of our Saviour throws a perfectly clear light upon this matter, seeing that His Soul was afflicted with a mortal sadness, while at the same time He was in the enjoyment of glory. This sadness, said St. Francis de Sales, caused that good Saviour to pray to His Father that, if it were possible, this bitter chalice might pass from Him, adding immediately, " Nevertheless, not as I will, but as You wilt":1 whence it is evident that our Lord was afflicted, not only in the sensitive part of His Soul, which does not possess a will, but also in the inferior reasonable part. Jesus, then, possessed ineffable joy in the superior part of His Soul at the same time that He was suffering agonies the greatest ever endured: the which clearly shows that joy in the superior region of the soul may be allied with the most painful interior states. And all the time that our good Master was so forsaken of His Father that He complained of it aloud, is it not certain that the glory of Hi a Soul was unaltered, and that He was in possession of the joy of the Beatific Vision? Consequently it must be allowed that the constant rejoicing to which the Apostle exhorts is none other than that which resides in the superior part of the soul by an entire conformity with the Divine Will; a joy which is often indefinable, and in no wise perceptible; which therefore leaves the soul in desolation, so that in many states it is not even cognizant whether it is resigned to the good pleasure of God, not knowing what is passing in its depth, all reflective acts being taken away from it. This joy was undoubtedly possessed by those holy persons who endured interior pains even to their death, but because it was not perceptible, they received no consolation from it.

But it will be further alleged that many persons create for themselves imaginary states of supernatural pains, or bring sufferings upon themselves by their own fault and imprudence. The answer is easy: that these abuses or faults ought to be avoided; that we do not approve of them; but the abuses which are to be met with in the holiest states, or the faults which lire committed therein, do not detract from the perfection and excellence of those states themselves. As for the abuses, we must get rid of them by the help of God's grace; and as regards the faults, we must be sorry for them, but nevertheless we must endure with patience the pains they entail, making a holy use of them. All the souls which are in Purgatory are there on account of their faults and their sins; the pains they endure they have brought upon themselves by their offences; but this does not prevent its being a very great happiness for them to undergo this purgation, in order to enjoy the Vision of God.

It will still be objected that consolations are good, and that sensible lights are gifts of God. All this is true: but it is also certain that they are dangerous, on account of human nature. It could not be denied without error that natural possessions are good in themselves: as, for example, gold and silver, lands, vineyards, and such-like things, which constitute the riches of the present life; and moreover, that they are the gifts of God; yet for all this the Son of God has declared Himself clearly in respect to these goods, and has pronounced Woe to those who possess them, because of the danger which attends them; and He has made happiness to consist in the endurance of poverty, which is a deprivation of those goods. Now apply this to spiritual consolations, which are the riches with which self-love regales itself. We do not say that these consolations are a bad thing; on the contrary, we say that they are useful and even necessary to some souls as aids to their feebleness; we allow that God gives them sometimes to very great saints; and that those on whom they are bestowed ought to receive them with thankfulness, as rich persons should do in the case of their temporal goods, and make a holy use of them, without becoming attached to them.

But, to say the truth, the happiness of the present life consists rather in their deprivation than in their enjoyment. In the first place, as has been said, by reason of the danger of self-love, which easily insinuates itself therein. Our Lord, speaking to a holy person, told her that He ought to be thanked far more for afflictions than for consolations, because consolations intoxicate the soul with vanity and pride; and that for a thousand who are lost in the way of afflictions, ten thousand perish in that of sensible consolations, which are the aliment of self-love. Secondly, the devil often mixes himself up therewith. There was a woman whose consolations were so abundant that she was quite transported beyond herself, and was accustomed to cry out that she could endure no more: but it was revealed by the Blessed Virgin that it was the devil from whom these consolations came; and she said that when a soul allows itself to be dilated with joy in these ways, the devil gets near, and confuses the mind with many thoughts and affections which have their source in self-love. In the third place, these consolations retard the soul's advance in the path of perfection. The case of one who is in these ways pretty much resembles that of a traveler who, having a long journey to go, instead of proceeding straight on, amuses himself with admiring the fine houses and beautiful gardens on the road, which his curiosity leads him to inspect. It is not so with him who on his journey meets with nothing but ugly and unsightly places; he walks without stopping: and is it not true that he arrives the sooner of the two at the place to which he is going, and to which his business calls him? In the fourth place, there is more love of God, generally speaking, in the privation of sensible lights and satisfactions, for there is less in them of the creature. I have treated more fully of this in my book, On the Reign of God in Mental Prayer; here I will only repeat what St Catherine of Genoa declared on this subject: "One means [of advancing] which pleases me most," said this saint, " is when God causes a man's mind to be filled with pain and affliction, in such wise that nature finds nothing to feed upon, and must needs consume itself. In consolations, creatures set themselves between God and us; in afflictions, God places Himself between us and creatures, in order to separate us from them. Our Lord said to a holy soul that prayers were more pleasing to Him when they were offered amid dryness, trouble, sadness, and repugnance. But, in a word, has not Scripture told us (Mark 9:5) that St. Peter knew not what he was saying when he said it was good to abide in the consolation of Thabor? And yet the divine splendors that were there manifested, and the delights that were there tasted, were most good and most excellent, since they were a reflection of the splendors and the floods of glory of Paradise, and of the glory of the very Saviour Himself.

After all, the Adorable Jesus is the true pattern of all the elect, and His divine life the rule of the life of all those who shall be saved. If we cast our eyes, then, on this adorable model, we shall see in it nothing but crosses: exterior crosses, terrible; interior crosses, immeasurably great. All His holy life was passed in suffering; for either He was actually enduring exterior pains, or His mind was afflicted with the ever-present vision of them; and that with such a faithful attachment to the Cross, that even on Thabor, when the Glory He received sent a deluge of joy through all the faculties of His soul, inferior as well as superior, so that its effects extended to His very garments, instead of allowing His mind to dwell upon it, He turns away His thoughts, and fixes them only on the torments of His Passion, to teach us emphatically that sensible joys are not suited for this life: you would say that He desired to efface from the minds of His disciples the sight of the glory He had shown them, for immediately He begins discoursing to them of nothing but the ignominious sufferings of His Cross. In fine, that assertion of the great Apostle (Rom. 15:3) is a general one: " Christ did not please Himself." " This proposition is a universal proposition," says the Reverend Father Louis Chardon, the Dominican, in his excellent book, The Cross of Jesus, a work which cannot be too much commended: " it includes, therefore, His understanding, mind, judgment, memory, all His rich endowments, and treasures of knowledge, from which He never permitted Himself to derive any satisfaction. It includes, moreover, the complacence He might have had in the ineffable union of His Holy Soul with One of the Three Divine Persons." What thought could be conceived more ravishing and transporting? And yet He refuses the unspeakable joy which He might have received from the Beatific Vision, to embrace in preference the thought of the confusion of the Cross, which takes possession of one portion of His mind. " Nay, even when dying," observes the same author, " His love of the Cross does not die: His Side will be opened by a thrust of a spear; it is His will that the Divine Eucharist should be a perpetual representation of His Passion; and because the Sacrifice must terminate with the world, He preserves His Wounds for all eternity,—Wounds that were wide enough to receive, not the fingers only, but the hands of His Apostles, to show us that His affection for the Cross can never cease.

I know that some say that it was necessary for the Adorable Jesus to be thus crucified, because He was the Saviour of mankind, and had come to make satisfaction for their sins. But, O my God, how absurd and irrational are the thoughts of men! If it was necessary that He who is Innocence Itself should suffer, ought the guilty one to lead a life of pleasures? If the Well-Beloved Son of the Eternal Father, Very God as He was, because He had taken the likeness of the sinner, and in his name had presented Himself before His Father, was overwhelmed beneath the torrents of His wrath and deluged with sufferings, ought the slave of the devil, who deserves only the wrath of God and the torments of hell, to be exempt from suffering? O strange, inconceivable reasoning! The Master, the Lord, the Son, the King—yea, God Himself must suffer; but as for the slave, the subject, the creature, the very nothing, the sinner who is less than nothing—this is no concern of his: joy and the sweetness of life are his portion.

Further, I would ask these persons, if the Cross is not the great grace of the present life, how is it that the Son of God suffered so much, and suffered to such an excess that life was a heavy burden to Him, as it is related in the fourteenth chapter of St. Mark (v. 33,34), seeing that the least of His pains was sufficient to satisfy for millions of worlds? This superfluity of crosses is an infallible testimony to His love for sufferings. And again I ask them, how it is that the most holy Virgin was plunged, as it were, into a boundless ocean of sorrows, and endured more than all the Saints? I ask them how it is that Holy Church sings, "What torments all the Saints have suffered!" Yet the Blessed Virgin, who never either contracted or committed the slightest sin, could not have suffered in order to be purified from her stains, seeing she was purer than the sun, yea, purer than the Angels: evident proof that states of suffering are designed, not only for the purification of souls, but for their more perfect sanctification. Finally, I ask them, Of whom shall we learn the ways of Heaven, if it be not from Him who is the Way, the Truth, and the Life?
Assuredly, if He had deemed, in His infinite wisdom, that there were anything better in this world than suffering, He would have taught it us by His example. This thought is taken from that divine book, The Following of Christ. That which so many miracles were unable to effect He accomplished by the Cross: proof, therefore, that the Cross contains something greater than all that is most marvelous and most miraculous in this life.

But let us listen to this Divine Master speaking to all His disciples: " If any man will come after Me, let him deny himself, and take up his cross " (Matt- 16:24). He does not say, " Have high contemplations, brilliant lights, spiritual consolation and joys "; all He asks is the Cross; and, to refute beforehand the subterfuge of those who say that the cross is good for a certain time, He does not limit His injunction to particular ages, conditions, or interior states, but declares to all His followers, without exception, that they must take up the cross: nay, to remove all doubt, one of the Evangelists (Luke 9:23) relates that He said they must take up their cross "daily." This declaration is clear and precise; and, indeed, its truth is obvious, since the same Divine Master affirms (John 20:21) that as His Father sent Him, so He sends us. If, then, He was sent to suffer, we are also in this world in order to endure. Let those who would throw the whole burden of suffering on our good Saviour reflect on this passage, which is expounded by the holy Fathers and spiritual writers as I have expounded it.

In fine, are we wiser than Wisdom Itself? The Son of God judged that His Father would be more glorified by the ways of the Cross than by ways of pleasantness: why should we not share His sentiments? Christianity itself was founded in this spirit. All reforms and all the great designs of God are accomplished by this means alone. Salvation is compared in Scripture to a mountain, because we must toil in order to attain it. Its way is narrow, yea, very narrow: whence it is plain- that it can be trodden only with difficulty. Complete security is found therein, but so also are toil and trouble. It is "a faithful saying," wrote the great Apostle (2 Tim. 2:11): " If we be dead with Jesus, we shall live also with Him." But do you not observe the condition? This is why he speaks (Col. 3:3) of all Christians being " dead." I will conclude, then, with these words, which the Son of God addressed to St. Teresa:—" Happiness in this world does not consist in the enjoyment of Me, but in serving Me, laboring for My glory, and suffering after My example."

Be not surprised, therefore, if this great saint took for her maxim, "Either to suffer or to die": as if she had meant to say, as soon as we cease to suffer in this world we must leave it, the Cross being here our great affair. Neither let us marvel if St. Catherine of Siena chose the crown of thorns, and preferred it to all others.

CHAPTER VI.

CROSSES ARE A MARK OF PREDESTINATION, AND OF A HIGH PREDESTINATION.

O Eternity, O Eternity, how small a place do You hold in the mind of men! Their blindness is so deplorable, that they are wholly immersed in the thought of that which is passing away, and concern themselves with nothing so little as with that which is eternal. It is true also that Eternity occupies but slightly even those souls which are most penetrated with the thought of it, for all men are unable to comprehend it; nevertheless it is also true that it will comprehend all men. O Eternity, all men will enter Your fathomless abysses, never more to leave them. O my soul, here are great truths which nearly concern us, of which we shall have experience, and that in no long time. Soon we shall pass into that Eternity—after the few years that remain to us, if, indeed, any yet remain. Will it be into a happy or an unhappy Eternity? This it is we do not know. O appalling uncertainty! I behold the pillars of heaven tremble thereat; I see those who are to judge the world turn pale with fear. But tremble as we may—let ceaseless floods of tears flow from our eyes—thither we must go.

O my soul, yet a little while,—I say it again—and we must pass into Eternity.
This, then, is a matter in which we must take our measures

with the strictest caution: to err therein is to be lost beyond recovery. Ah, the terrible thought: it is certain damnation! We find doctors and holy Fathers furnishing us with signs of predestination, that is to say, with marks by which we may know whether we shall attain to a blessed Eternity. They offer many which command our profound respect, and which are well fitted to bring consolation. But let us listen to Him who cannot be deceived, and who cannot deceive, the Holy Spirit, the Spirit of Truth. Assuredly the things which He reveals are infallible.

I hear Him, then, saying in the Scripture (Gal. 5:24), " They that are Christ's have crucified their flesh, with the vices and concupiscences." O my soul, to belong to Christ, therefore, one must be crucified.

I hear Him saying (John 12:25), " He that hates his life in this world, keeps it unto life eternal." Here He teaches us that to be saved we must hate ourselves; and so certain is this, that, to remove all doubt, He declares that " he that loves his life shall lose it." I hear Him saying (Rom. 8:29) that the elect are they whom the Eternal Father " predestinated to be made conformable to the image of His Son." The true mark of predestination, then, is to be found in the likeness which we bear to this Well Beloved Son. Let us fix our eyes, let us keep them fixed, on this Divine Original, that we may become true copies of It; and let us from time to time examine ourselves to see if we resemble It. This ought to be our rule in the matter of our salvation. You who read this, take heed thereto. Are you like to Jesus Christ? O my soul, I who write these truths —am I like unto Him? "There came," says Holy Scripture (Mark 1:11), "a voice from Heaven: 'Thou are My Beloved Son'; and immediately the Spirit drove Him out into the desert"; and He was there with the beasts, as St. Mark relates (vv. 12, 13). No sooner does Heaven declare the Adorable Jesus to be the Well Beloved Son of the Eternal Father, than He begins to suffer. But alas! His whole life was only one continual Cross. If the Son of God be requested that His beloved disciple, the Evangelist St. John, may sit beside Him in His kingdom, He asks (Matt. 20:22) if he can drink of His chalice. This is the necessary condition, from which not even His most favored ones are exempted. Benjamin, in the Old Law, was the figure of the predestinate: accordingly, it is to him that the cup, or chalice, is given—a gift, says St. Ambrose, which is presented to only one of all the children of Jacob. To all, indeed, corn was given; but the chalice is reserved for one alone. In fine the great Doctor of our salvation, the Adorable Jesus, teaches us (John 16:20) that His disciples shall lament and weep, but the world shall rejoice, that world which knows not God and is the enemy of God. It is not possible to give plainer marks of salvation. Lamentation and tears, according to the doctrine of a God-Man, are the portion of the predestinate.

But are these marks so certain and so general as to belong to all the elect? Of this there can be no doubt; since the Holy Spirit distinctly assures us, in the Epistle to the Hebrews (12:6), that God chastises and scourges all His children. He who says all excepts none. And to leave the human mind no room for subterfuge, He calls (v. 8) those who are without chastisements " bastards, and not sons." Is it possible for Scripture to speak more clearly? Hence St. Augustine does not hesitate to say that he who is not in the number of those who suffer is not numbered among the children of God; that we must not hope for the inheritance of salvation without having a share of the Cross; that it is to deceive ourselves greatly, to wish to exempt ourselves from the pains of this life, seeing that none of the elect have been thus exempt. " Will you listen?" says this Father. " God has but one Son by nature, who is Innocence Itself, and who is without sin: yet He was not exempted from the law of suffering." A holy bishop, who was deeply penetrated with this truth, met with a man who told him that he had always lived in honour and comfort, in the enjoyment of good health, amid an abundance of earthly possessions, and surrounded by a family that had known nothing but prosperity. "Ah!" Exclaimed that prelate, " these are all great signs of the anger of God; let us fly with all speed from a house where no crosses to be seen." Scarcely had he quit it when the wrath of God fell on that man and on his family, who were all buried under the ruins of their house.

Further, it must be said that crosses are the marks, not only of predestination, but of a high predestination. This is clearly manifested in the person of our Lord, in the most holy Virgin, and the greatest Saints, who, having been exalted to the highest sanctity, have been loaded with the heaviest crosses. Those living stones, with which the Almighty builds the Heavenly Jerusalem, are, as the Church sings, " polished by the hammer" of affliction. Now, in this great city of the Heavenly Jerusalem, all the predestinate have each their own particular mansion, the building of which requires more or less labour in proportion to what its extent and elevation are to be. The small degree of labour undergone in commencing and completing a mansion is an evident mark of its being no great thing. Courage, then, O my soul, in your sufferings; all your pains serve only to the increase of your glory. See you all these who combine to make you suffer: these demons who assail 'you so furiously; these bad men, who persecute you so unjustly; these good people, who take part therein, thinking they are doing right; these friends, who desert you; these relatives, who cast you off? They are all so many workmen who are laboring to make glorious crowns for you. Oh, what good workmen, and how lovable, if you truly know what they are doing, and if you regard them with the eyes of faith and not with eyes of flesh! Oh, blessed are they who weep! Let us abide by the sentiments of a God, no matter what may be the judgment of creatures. O my soul, what happy tidings! we shall reign—yes, we shall reign with the Great King, Jesus, if we also suffer with Him.

CHAPTER VII

CROSSES EXALT TO MATCHLESS GLORY.

Oh, why do not the ambitious men of this world understand this truth! What a change would come over their spirit and dispositions; and how they would trample under foot all earthly splendor, to aspire henceforth only after the glory of the Cross! Yes, we maintain,, with the most enlightened of the Saints, that there is no glory which can compare with it. This truth is set forth in a manner truly admirable by the golden mouth of the eloquent St. John Chrysostom. You would say that Heaven had poured into the mind of this great prelate of Constantinople all the richest illuminations of the Cross, because it destined him to the most afflicting sufferings. All the most hidden mysteries of the Cross are manifested to him. It is given to him to penetrate into the very depths of its most divine secrets, because he is himself to pass along its most rugged ways, and to serve as a finished model of patience to all posterity. The following are the sentiments of this saintly man on the incomparable glory of sufferings. In the first place, if among the most exalted honours of the world there is nothing more resplendent than the diadems of monarchs, he declares that suffering is something grander than the empire of the universe, and that all who suffer in a Christian spirit are great kings. Secondly, if the titles of Apostle and Evangelist rank highest among the dignities of the Kingdom of Jesus

Christ, he protests that the glory of the Apostle and of the sacred writer must yield to that of sufferings; that it is more honourable to be loaded with chains for the sake of Jesus Christ, than to bear the title of Evangelist or that of Teacher of the World. In the third place, he declares that he would willingly leave Heaven itself, if the choice were given him, in order to suffer for the God of Heaven; that he would prefer a dungeon to the loftiest thrones in the empyrean; that the very glory of the Seraphim would be less an object of desire to him than that of the most painful crosses. Hence he accounts St. Paul more happy in having been thrown into prison than in having been rapt even to the third heaven; and he prefers the ignominy of the Prince of the Apostles, bound with chains, to the happiness of the blessed spirit who comes to set him free. In the fourth place, he goes further, and does not hesitate to say that he prefers being hardly treated by Jesus Christ, by being made a sharer in His Cross, to being honoured by that King of Heaven and Earth. In the fifth place, observing that the gift of miracles attracts the veneration of all peoples, he affirms that to command demons, to give impulse and motion to the elements, to stay the sun in its course, are all things inferior to the honour of sufferings. And, in truth, the great St. Augustine justly estimates what the Gospel says (John 7:39) of the Holy Spirit not yet being given because Jesus was not glorified, and this, too, at the time that He was performing the most admirable miracles. " Wonderful!" exclaims this Father: " Jesus was not glorified while He was manifesting His power over death by the resurrection of many whom He raised again to life; He is glorified when death is given power over Him and deprives Him of His life."

Is it not because of the ignominies and humiliations of that bitter death of our Divine Master that His Father has exalted Him, and has given Him a Name which is above all names, so that at the Name of Jesus all creatures in heaven, on earth, and under the earth should bow the knee? Is it not on this account that He calls (John 12:23) the hour of His death the hour of His glory? This being so, let us no longer be surprised if Saints make the highest honour of this present life to consist in the lowest abasements. St. Paul takes (Eph. 3:1) for one of his most honourable titles that of " Paul the prisoner," or captive; and he places (Gal. 6:14) his greatest glory in the infamy of the Cross endured for his Master's sake.

I ask you, then, you who read these truths, what are you doing? You have seen what the King of Saints and His greatest saints have done; but what do you see in yourselves? Examine for a while, in the presence of God, what your sentiments are in respect to these crosses. Do you regard yourself, when bearing them, as a great king; as one whose sufferings are reckoned of more account by Apostles and Evangelists than their own titles, which give them the highest rank in the Church? Do you look upon yourself as one whose state might inspire Seraphim with envy, if they were capable of it, and renders you more glorious than if you raised the dead? If this be so, why are you sad? Why are you impatient when you suffer? Are you disposed to murmur at having a scepter put into your hand and a crown upon your head, and having honours paid to you which even monarchs cannot claim? O poor, afflicted, rejected, forsaken creature, who are treated as the refuse of the earth, take comfort and rejoice. Rejoice, You poor man, who have not a morsel of bread: yet a little, only a little more patience, and before the eyes of all mankind, yea, and of Your own, which in this world are so often closed to these divine lights, You shalt see Yourself exalted to an incomparable glory. "Of what, then, are You afraid?"

says St. Ambrose; "they who are afraid of being tried and afflicted are afraid of being crowned."

CHAPTER VIII.

CROSSES ARE THE EARTHLY PARADISE.

Many have been the inquiries instituted respecting the site of the earthly Paradise; and very fruitlessly Now, without so many investigations, behold it ready found. There is no need to go far to make so blessed a discovery. Have you found suffering, you have found the earthly Paradise. This assertion will, perhaps, at first sight appear surprising, but its truth is none the less certain. No one can deny that there is no other real Paradise save God alone, and that it is only in union with Him that the soul finds its perfect happiness. It is an incontestable truth as regards both Heaven and earth: with this difference, however, that union with God in Heaven is at its term; it is no longer capable of increase, and is exempt from all suffering and that, on the contrary, union with God in this life can increase and be augmented more and more; though this is not effected without difficulty, on account of the obstacles to be encountered. Now, as crosses are the great means which remove out of our way the impediments to divine union, by withdrawing us from the created being to unite us to the Increate, it may well be said that they are the earthly Paradise, since by them we are united to God alone, our center and our end.

This is why we say that the happiness of the present life consists in sufferings, because by them we arrive at the enjoyment of God in a manner more pure and perfect. True it is, that often the sweetness of this happiness is not tasted by the senses, or perceived in the inferior reasonable portion of the soul, lest self-love and personal satisfaction should be mixed therewith; but this blessedness is none the less really possessed by the soul, which enjoys its true happiness when it abides in its centre, that is to say, in union with its God. This it clearly sees when its Sovereign is pleased to make this manifestation to it; which He does sometimes with sensible sweetness so delightful, or, if the senses have no part therein, with lights so vivid and so clear, that, in the midst of crosses the most afflicting to nature, the soul seems to have a foretaste of the joy of the blessed.

And yet this sensible sweetness and these intellectual lights are but flashes of grace on the sensitive portion of the soul, or a certain reflected perception of the blessing which it possesses; namely, union with God alone. Now, this union in the present life is often so much the purer and more perfect as it is the less known. Provided only that we remain closely united to our centre, we do in fact possess and enjoy this felicity. And here we may discern the reason why holy souls have been plunged in such profound sadness when the crosses which afflicted them were on the point of being withdrawn. Sometimes even they have been sorely perplexed as to whence so extraordinary a sadness could proceed; for commonly a feeling of joy is experienced at being delivered from suffering. The reason is that these souls, from having found their happiness in union with God alone by means of crosses, and knowing that they were about to lose this means, were possessed with the fear lest, in being deprived of it, they should lose the perfect enjoyment of their centre. We say further, that it is pleasanter to suffer than to think of suffering. This may also appear strange, and yet it is most true. The reason is that the thought of suffering does not unite us to God alone, as actual suffering does. The road which leads to the place we are going to is the necessary means for reaching it; but there is a great difference between the thought of setting off on our road and actually doing so. You see plainly that the thought of going to a place does not take us there: in like manner, sentiments, views, or thoughts about crosses do not conduct us to union with God alone, as do crosses themselves, and consequently do not enable us to enjoy the happiness which is found in that union, as actual sufferings do. O Christian soul, do what You will, turn which way You may—though You should enjoy all the honors, pleasures, and riches of the world—you wilt never find Your rest save in God alone: God alone is Your beginning, Your center, and Your end. Look now at this man who has made a false step and dislocated one of his limbs: he cries out from the great pain he is enduring. Well, suppose someone should say to him, " Eh! My poor man, why do you cry out? You have broken no bone; neither your leg nor your foot is fractured?" "Ah!" He would reply, "very true; but the bone is out of its place, and that is quite enough to cause me great pain." If, then, a bone out of its proper place is capable of causing so much suffering—oh, what must we think of a soul which is out of union with God? But what a blessed thing is the Cross, seeing that it has such power to lead us thereto, maintains us therein so securely, and enables us to enjoy it more and more in a manner so holy!

I knew a sick person, who found himself much relieved from a feverish headache by meditating on the blessedness of crosses; and this is the mode in which he exercised his mind upon it: He imagined himself entirely forsaken by creatures, the victim of repeated persecutions, robbed of his reputation, and of everything he held dearest in the world. He thought of himself as deserted by his friends, ill spoken of by good people and God's servants, opposed on all hands, and treated as an outcast on earth. Then he beheld himself in such an utter state of abandonment, that, when reduced to the last extremity of sickness, he could not find even a stable to retreat to, or a glass of water in his sorest need, or a single person to assist him, but was forced to die in the open street, in a gutter, like a wretched dog. As he meditated in this wise, he experienced great relief, and said, " This is indeed the earthly Paradise: if there be any happiness in the world, it is this." In course of time the person in question actually experienced in a large measure what at that time he had only thought of; and I heard him say, while actually under the trial, that he was very far from having changed his opinion: on the contrary, he had learned a hundred thousand times better that the happiness of this present life consists in much suffering. O God Only, God Only, God Only!

A PRAYER, TO THE BLESSED VIRGIN, QUEEN OF ALL THE HOLIEST LIGHTS OF GRACE.

O Sacred Virgin, You are as a divine aurora in the dawn of Your immaculate conception, all pure and all holy; You are as a fair moon in the progress of Your admirable life; and, again, You are of surpassing brightness, like the sun, not only because You are all clothed with the Sun of Justice, and wholly penetrated with the lights of grace and the ineffable flames of His pure love, but also because, as the visible sun in the heavens brings day to the world below, so it is for You that the Invisible Sun sheds His rays on all the world of grace. O sacred Virgin, obtain for me, and for those who shall read this little work, which is all thine, as is whatever else I have, some special share in the lights of Your Beloved Son, so that we may ever hold the Cross in high esteem, and thence derive so true a love as may serve to unite us with the Most Holy Trinity, Father, Son, and Holy Ghost Amen.

PART II.

EXTERIOR TRIALS.

CHAPTER I

THE WAYS OF THE CROSS ARE VARIOUS.

Indisputable as it is that the true disciples of the Son of God all bear their crosses, after the pattern and following in the steps of their Divine Master, nevertheless it is quite certain that all do not bear them in an equal degree. All walk by the way of the Cross, but after a very different manner. Some are conducted along it by exterior sufferings, others by interior. You will see some who are tried by corporal maladies; others you will see who are afflicted with the loss of their brightest intellectual gifts, and even of their mind itself, as has befallen some of the greatest men who have ever lived, and other servants of God. There are those who have been reduced to great poverty, by the loss of a lawsuit or by other disasters, or who have been in a destitute condition from their birth. And again there are those who suffer from being deprived of their earthly happiness, of their offices and employments. Others are persecuted by their fellow-creatures: they meet with nothing but contradictions on every side, and that from good men as well as from bad; their reputation is torn to pieces, and they are assailed with calumnies on all hands. Others are grievously tormented by devils. And again there are those who are strangely crucified by interior pains, which vary much in their nature, according to the disposition of Divine Providence. You will meet with persons who have been completely abandoned by those who were under obligations to them; by friends, relatives, and those, too, the most nearly allied. A wife will suffer much from a husband, a husband from a wife, a father from a child.

Now there are some of these crucified souls who bear several of these crosses all at once; who are sorely tried on all sides, by Heaven and by earth, by men and by demons, both exteriorly and interiorly. There are crosses which, though light in themselves, are most heavy to those who bear them, and cause them great suffering; while there are others which in themselves are very heavy, but which become quite light because Grace makes them easy. There are persons who excite compassion by the frightful evils they endure, yet interiorly they are overflowing with joy: so that they suffer almost without suffering. Others, again, you will meet with whose afflictions are so light that their best friends only laugh at them, no one thinks there is any call to pity them; nevertheless their sufferings are extreme. After all, although it is true that the Christian has always to bear the Cross during the whole course of his life, since he always has to combat and is always liable to sin—for even though he were confirmed in grace, that privilege would not exempt from venial faults—nevertheless God in dealing with certain souls intermingles many consolations. There are souls to whom pain has become scarcely any pain at all. But in all these different ways we must adore, love, bless, praise, and render thanks, with entire submission to the disposition of Divine Providence; taking good care never curiously to scan or examine why God leads some in one way and some in another way. In this abyss the created mind would lose itself. God is the Absolute Master; it is the duty of the creature to hold itself in an entire dependence on His behests, to adore them and love them, to keep a profound and most respectful silence, and never be guilty of such insolent rashness as to ask Him, Why do you do this? Down with the human spirit, down with all human reasoning, in the presence of God! Otherwise we shall but make ourselves a road to go straight to Hell, to be damned eternally with those evil spirits whose pride brought them there. I do not say that we can prevent a number of thoughts which arise involuntarily in the mind, but we must not dwell upon them with set determination of the will.

However, there are some crucified souls whom God delivers from the opprobrium of the world, and whose innocence He vindicates, not even sparing miracles for this end; but others there are whose innocence always remains oppressed, who live and die upon their crosses, and are even persecuted after their death. This is exemplified in many Saints, who have endured interior pains all their life, or have continued to be the victims of calumny, their memory being assailed after they were dead. To all this we may say, that these latter are the happier, because they are in closest conformity with our Lord, whose whole life was one of suffering, poverty, and contempt; who, being Innocence Itself, was never justified before men, but, on the ground of the accusations brought against His Divine Person, was judged and condemned before all sorts of tribunals, ecclesiastical and lay—by kings and governors of provinces, by the chief pontiff, by the priests and doctors of the law; who would not work a miracle, when on the Cross, in His own vindication, although men told Him that they would believe in Him if He did; who would not perform any to deliver His most holy Mother and St. Joseph from their poverty and afflictions. True, He has wrought many for the relief of a number of Saints; but He dealt not thus with His own Divine Person, His holy Mother, St. Joseph, or St. John Baptist, whom, as regarded the goods of this life, He left to the ordinary course of things. Moreover, this God-Man has been pleased, after His death and in the midst of His triumphs, still to suffer by the sins of Christians, by the prevarication of heretics, by the unbelief of Mahometans and pagans; He has exposed His Body to frightful ignominies in the Most Holy Sacrament, by permitting the senses to have no cognizance of anything save the appearance of bread; He suffers by being daily blasphemed, despised, contradicted, rejected—driven from minds and hearts, and, exteriorly, from so many provinces and kingdoms, out of which heresy has banished the Divine Eucharist. After this, can we be astonished if among His elect there are those whom He destines to suffer during their whole life, and even after their death? To the day of the great general judgment, at the end of the world, is reserved the manifestation of all things, and the recompense or punishment, publicly and before all the peoples of the earth, of virtue and of vice.

CHAPTER II.

EVERY ONE MUST BEAR HIS OWN CROSS, AND IN THE MANNER GOD WILLS.

After speaking of so many different crosses, what remains for us to do but to take up our own, that cross which it has pleased Divine Providence to give us? How explicit is our Master on this subject, when He says (Matt. 16:24), " If any man will come after Me, let him take up his cross"! For He does not say, "Let him take up the cross," but " his cross." It is, then, an indisputable truth that everyone must bear his own cross. O my soul! See You this Divine King of the predestinate, at the head of His elect, loaded with the heaviest Cross there ever was, and which includes within it all the crosses of the Saints? If You take note of all His following, You will not see one of those who have belonged to Him from the beginning of the world, who has not borne his own cross: and so it will be to the end of time. We must, then, resolutely bear our cross: and how, indeed, can we do otherwise? Is it possible that we could be so demented as to imagine that we alone should be exempted from the life common to all the predestinate? No, no: there is no room for doubt in a matter which is certain, to the last degree of certainty. Everyone must bear his own cross.

I will speak at large, in the fourth book of this little work, on the way of bearing it well; but I will say something here as to what we must avoid, and what we must do. And I will commence by saying that there are three things of which we must beware.

The first is not to procure ourselves crosses by our own faults or by our imagination, figuring to ourselves states of suffering, because we have read of them or heard of them, or because we have allowed them to occupy our thoughts too much. When you have committed faults, be sorry for them, but do not distress yourself; and as for the imagination, try quietly to apply a remedy, by diverting it from the subject of its application, and following such advice as experienced persons will give you. This done, disturb yourself no further; and be assured once for all that any effects which proceed from your sins, or from your imagination, and which have ceased to be voluntary in you, are crosses which God wills that you shall bear. Be not depressed, then, by your sufferings because you have brought them on yourself; but take courage and be comforted: God, who did not will the cause, wills the effect. I have already said, and peradventure I shall say it again: Have the pains of Purgatory any other cause but sin? Do like those holy souls who suffer therein: endure in peace, with placidity and tranquility of soul.

The second thing we must avoid is not to amuse ourselves by desiring other crosses than those we have. You will see persons who never reflect well on what they have, but are always thinking of what they have not. They occupy themselves with the sufferings of others, and fancy that they would be better suited to themselves than their own; they are very far from desiring—so they say—not to bear the cross: oh, no; but they would prefer other crosses to those which have been laid upon them. They imagine they would make quite a different use of them, and would not allow themselves to fall into the faults which they now commit. All this is nothing but self-love and presumption. Do we think to be wiser than Eternal Wisdom, and to know better what crosses are suitable for us than does God Himself? O what folly, what rashness! Believe me, we know nothing about the matter. If we were left to ourselves, we should make ourselves crosses which would be either too long or too short, too heavy or too light. It belongs to Jesus alone to shape them to our proper measure. Hold it for certain that the one you have, whatever your senses or your judgment may say, is the very one which suits you. Let this suffice; and think only of making a good use of your cross. The devil is deluding you, lest it should be of benefit to you: he makes you think of other crosses with which you have nothing to do, and forget that which belongs to you. After all, are you not wasting time? What good is all this doing you?

The third thing which we must avoid is that subtle device of self-love which suggests that it is quite right we should bear our own cross, but that it would be desirable it should be borne in some different way. We are content to have the suffering in itself, but should be glad to have it after another fashion. All this is mere delusion. We must bear our own cross, and bear it in the way God gives it. It is the will of God to which we must look, and not precisely the cross itself, seeing that it is God's will we are to do herein,

75

and not our own. Bear in mind that the Cross of our Lord, I mean that which we ought to bear as Christians, does not exactly consist in much fasting, watching, and suffering; for the devils never eat or sleep, and suffer unutterable torments. Neither does it exactly consist in depriving ourselves of our goods to give them to the poor, and living in poverty; for the great Apostle declares (1 Cor. 13:3) that this may be done without profit, and without the true love of God. Nor, again, does it consist in solitude, for how many shepherds are there who are bad men, and yet lead solitary lives! It consists, then, in suffering borne in the spirit of Jesus Christ, because He wills that we should suffer as we do. Now this cannot be done unless we suffer in the manner He ordains.

Moreover, turn all your crosses to the best account. Oh! How good it is in this matter to be a careful manager. That anchorite was a wonderful man who, seeing the worms fall from his half-putrid flesh, carefully picked them up and applied them to other parts of his body. He was afraid of losing the smallest of them. Lose not, then, the smallest occasion of suffering; do not let the least of those happy moments slip away; have a holy greed in this matter. Do you see that man who is so attached to this world's goods? To take a ten-franc piece from him would be like tearing his heart out. Oh, what would be his delight if one showed him a treasure, out of which he had full liberty to draw for a whole day together, and take handfuls of gold and silver! I warrant you he would not lose a moment; and he would be a clever man who should draw him away to anything else. But know you not that the treasure of sufferings contains boundless riches of glory? If you had a morsel of the True Cross, and you let a few particles fall on the ground, immediately you would throw yourself upon your knees to gather them up; you would look all about, for fear of losing the smallest fragment; you would call your children to help you in the search. Ah! The crosses you bear are also the filling-up of the Cross of our good Saviour. Have a care, then, to let none of them escape you.

To this end, once again, look well to the will of God in your crosses. See God in them; look upon temptation, not as suggested by the evil spirit, but as coming by God's appointment for your particular good. Do the same in everything that happens to you, either on the part of men or from natural causes, be they maladies, losses, or other accidents. Do not behave like dogs, who run after the stone that is thrown for them without regarding the hand from which it comes: this is a homely and common-place comparison, but it is a useful one; apply it to yourself. O my God, shall we always look at second causes, without regarding the First Cause?

CHAPTER III.

WE MUST BEAR OUR CROSSES IN THE MANNER GOD WILLS.

" We pray God," says St. Teresa, " that His will may done, and when He sends us trials, which are an effect of His will, we desire it no longer." We must be faithful, therefore, in accepting crosses; but it is not enough to accept them; we must take them upon us with- a good courage, and not stay debating, consulting, and listening to our repugnance. " Why stand bargaining so long," says a spiritual writer, " about doing the work of God? We ought to throw ourselves," he continues, " into all God's designs, even without knowing what they are; and be well content not to know them: His will is enough; we must be satisfied to be stone-blind as respects our interior states."

The soul ought not only to be thus ignorant of its condition, but to be as nothing before the Most Adorable Being of God. To this end, we ought to avoid voluntary reflections and ratiocinations, to which women are more particularly subject. The devil mixes himself up into this, and then the excitement with which a person is bent on exploring his state, or resisting evil, so fills the mind with images of temptation that he may be said to become familiarized with them. A pretext is never wanting; for people will say that they reflect in order to discover whether they have consented to the temptation or not. But in the case of souls interiorly afflicted this is usually a stratagem of self-love and a movement of curiosity, as is also the repetition of genera] confessions. In all cases we ought to abide by the opinion of an experienced director, and remember that to persevere in good, two things are very necessary: to do it in spite of opposition; and to do it in the midst of the utmost conceivable darkness. Add to this, that we ought to divert our imagination quietly from dwelling on our sufferings, and avoid scrutinizing them, as also a certain tender compassion for ourselves, or that vain delusion of the mind which makes us believe that we are the most miserable persons in the world, and that there are few who suffer as we do. You meet with people of this sort who are never tired of talking about their crosses, who make a sort of property of them—for, strange to say, self- love finds an entrance sometimes even here—who exalt and value themselves on account of these crosses of theirs, and contemplate themselves upon them, and think they are doing something notable. Alas! We are not worthy of the crosses we have, and in the most arduous ways we have every reason for deep self-humiliation and fear, and a profound conviction of our own misery and nothingness.

One of the grand secrets for bearing well our cross is to rid ourselves of the disquietude it causes, and thus to suffer in tranquility, by an entire conformity to the Divine Will. It can never be too often repeated: disquietude is profitless; as much so as despondency and depression. Humble yourself deeply, for this is God's design; be not disquieted, for that is the devil's object. It is necessary, moreover (says a great prelate), not to give way to fear: the first step on the way to victory is confidence; and now I will teach you a stratagem of war: the devil, utterly impotent and reprobate as he is, has abated none of his pride; consequently he cannot endure contempt, and keeps aloof from such as do battle with him in that way.

Above all things, we must take notice that patience does not consist in being free from all disturbance, in experiencing no repugnance, or heaviness, or involuntary sadness, or in feeling no opposition to good, but in being willing to suffer in our interior whatever God wills, and in the manner He wills, in spite of all we may feel to the contrary. Many persons therefore are mistaken when they say that they are unwilling to suffer, because they experience so much aversion and sensible repugnance to suffering; for, if you thoroughly examined the inmost depth of their soul, you would find that they wish nothing but what God wills. The example of our Lord is very consoling on this point. He evinces heaviness and sadness: therefore it is allowable to lament ourselves. He prays His Father two or three times that the chalice may pass from Him: proof that the sensibility of the inferior part of the soul does not prevent an entire conformity to God's decrees. There have been great souls whose sensible sufferings compelled them to utter loud cries, and whose will nevertheless was wholly merged in that of God: and did not our Master Himself cry with a loud voice upon the Cross in His great dereliction by His Father?

Observe that often the efforts we make to free ourselves from the cross laid upon us are utterly useless. " There are persons suffering interior pains," says Tauler, " who, the more trouble they take and the greater efforts they make, are afflicted with all the greater dryness, and become as hard as stones, so that at times they have great difficulty in suffering with patience, and become more and more distressed and discouraged; besides which, you may detect a certain secret presumption, which makes them act as if it were possible to get the better of temptations by one's own efforts: which is the very way to increase them; for it nourishes pride, and our trials are sent to rid us of pride." Self-abandonment, therefore, complete and unreserved, is necessary in order to attain to a perfect indifference to suffering of every kind, in regard both to its intensity and its duration. Sometimes God waits only for this complete abandonment to give the sufferer relief, as we read in the case of the Venerable Brother Alphonsus Rodriguez, of the Company of Jesus. Self-will is the great cause of our sufferings: were it destroyed, oftentimes they would cease; but we need not be surprised if, the cause still remaining, the effects continue. Your pains are given you to purify you, and to detach you; at least this is one of their principal objects. You remain still attached to this or that wish in your crosses; how, then, can you expect them to cease? Do you not perceive that these personal wishes of yours supply fresh matter for suffering? Ah! How much better God knows what is needful for us than we do ourselves! Weigh well these truths. He sees what befalls us; He loves us more than we love ourselves; He could prevent it, and He does not prevent it. Of necessity, therefore, and without doubt, that which befalls us must be the best for us.

A little patience, then, a little courage, and recourse to the grace of our Lord; and, though our state should be quite desperate, according to human prudence, He will give us the victory. God never fails to bestow grace to suffer; if we succumb it is our own fault. Listen to what that eminent prelate, De Belley, says in his Spiritual Conflict, chapter 17th:—" This is an unquestionable truth, that God, who is faithful to His promises, never suffers us to be tempted above our strength; hence it follows of necessity that they who fall have not done all they might have done in the way of resistance; and when they seek excuses for their sin in their own weakness, we may stop their mouth by saying to them, Iniquity lies to itself; like those wicked ones who say in Wisdom (5:6), ' The light of Justice has not shined unto us.' God having done for the vineyard of their interior all that it needed, it is their own badness alone which yields thorns instead of grapes. How many saints, with less graces, have overcome greater temptations! No, no; God never refuses His aid to him who does what he ought."

Rely, then, on the assistance of the Lord, and tarry not to consider your own strength, which is nothing but feebleness. With Jesus we shall be able to do all things, we shall be able to overcome all that we most dread. Marvel not if you feel in yourself so little vigor to contend with the temptations which you foresee, or to endure tortures which might befall you. As the time is not yet come either for combating or for suffering, those great succors which will not fail you on the part of God are not yet afforded you: when, in their proper time, you shall receive them, the actual crosses laid upon you will cause you less fear than you now experience from the mere thought of them. When the hour of sacrifice arrives, stand firm under the trial; bear with yourself in the repugnance you may feel towards it, and even in the faults you may commit, bear all from the pure love of God alone, without looking for any consolation. Suffer with love, with joy, with thanksgiving, with astonishment at the honor that is done you in giving you a share in the Cross of the Son of God. Love with courage the Justice of God, which is God Himself, as well as His divine mercy and goodness. If you have but a little of pure love, yon will love this Justice, whatever it may cost you, and then you will be delighted that it should punish your faults, and will seek no diminution of your pains. An excellent director, seeing a soul tried with great suffering, said, " God wills it; that is enough: if I could relieve you of all your sufferings by the turn of a pin, I would not do it."

In fine, the devil, not being able to betray a soul into error in the way of sufferings, is glad at least to turn it away from its duties. Do not then, discontinue your spiritual exercises, or quit any occupation which concerns your vocation, on account of any weariness, sadness, disquietude, or distress which you may feel. "Do like those sick people," says a great prelate, " who in eating follow rather their reason than their appetite." Be also more assiduous in frequenting the sacraments, although you may perform all these things without relish, without feeling, and, as it seems to you, without fervor, but, on the contrary, with aversion, repugnance, disinclination, and an arduous effort of the mind.

CHAPTER IV.

CORPORAL INFIRMITIES.

Rejoice, you who are afflicted with bodily ailments.
St. Teresa blessed God because, not having a vigorous constitution, travelling made her feverish, and thus augmented her sufferings. She declared that a soul which is exercised by painful toils and illnesses is never dry, but

is always saturated with the Spirit of God. Rejoice, you who have bodily defects, whether you have had them from your birth, or that they are the result of some accident: you will on that account not be so agreeable to creatures, who, by not attaching themselves to you, will leave you more free to detach yourselves from them, that you may unite yourselves to God alone. O what a gracious favor to be thus ill favored by nature! In the next life what would we not wish that we had given to obtain those means which, by separating us from the creature, unite us to the Creator! Ah, how many, how very many souls are now groaning in hell because they were comely in person and had fine natural gifts! Ah, if you could hear them cursing what the world loves so much— this beauty, these natural charms! How many souls are saved because, being displeasing to creatures, they have attached themselves to God; or because, having a feeble and ailing body, they have been prevented from entangling themselves in the vanities of the world! I have known persons who declared to me that but for their bodily maladies they would be lost. Yet that holy book, The Following of Christ, affirms that few persons become better for the infirmities of sickness. The reason is that they do not make a Christian use of them. Make, then, a good use of these afflictions, and to this end learn that the grace of bodily ailments is a very great one. " God," says St. Catherine of Genoa, " converts the bodies of sick persons into a present Purgatory." Learn that it is so great a grace that it is sufficient to bring a soul to a high degree of sanctity, as we read of many saints, whose life was one of unceasing bodily ailment. What works did these persons so eminent for sanctity perform? Did they visit the poor? Did they preach? What were their exercises and employments except this—to be sick and ailing? Seek help from Heaven, that you may obtain the gift of great patience; it is very necessary in maladies which are attended with acute pains or which are of long duration. Remember that ailments which last a long time ought to be carefully utilized for Eternity; it is the occupation which Divine Providence assigns to persons thus tried for gaining Heaven. Let them give good heed to make a faithful use of them; for usually their prolonged duration renders them wearisome.

Further, keep a watch over the stratagems of self-love, which insinuates itself everywhere; it will not fail to furnish you in this case with a multitude of pretexts, wearing even a plausible coloring of the glory of God: in order to render your maladies irksome to you, it will suggest to your mind that your infirmities make you a burden to those you live with; but God who wills these infirmities wills all the consequences of them. We too, then, must will them, and not disquiet ourselves, although we may be a burden and a trouble to others. It will represent to you that you are useless in the world; and especially, if you live in a community, it will try to sadden you with the thought; but be assured that sick persons who are true Christians are not useless, as is imagined by those who look at things only with the eyes of the flesh. Oh, what sweet mercies do these suffering souls draw down from Heaven on the houses where they dwell; and how incomparably more good they do there than is done by those busy, active persons who have so many schemes and projects, and abound in natural resources, and who are generally regarded as the mainstays of communities! O my God, how differently do Your divine eyes look at things from the way in which they are viewed by the eyes of men who are wise with the world's wisdom! Never have communities been better provided for, both temporally and spiritually, than when they have had many truly crucified souls among them. Understand well this truth, ye superiors, and remember that your houses can never be more firmly established than upon the Cross.

Again, self-love will pretend that bodily ailments prevent persons from performing their spiritual exercises, and fulfilling the obligations of their community or vocation: as, for example, a preacher from preaching, a superior from discharging the duties of his office, an artisan from working at his trade. But how palpably flimsy are all such pretexts! I would ask you why you desire to do all these things, unless it be because God desires them: from the moment, then, that God desires them no longer, why should you wish to do them, unless it be to follow your own will, which is against all order and right? But one is prevented doing so much good, you will tell me. This again is a subterfuge of self-love. Are we to set ourselves to do the good which God does not wish us to do? Quite right, you will still reply; but I am a religious, a preacher, or an artisan. Truly, self-love is a strange beast, which it is not easy to kill, and which besides is always coming to life again. Does God not know that you are a religious, a preacher, an artisan? He knows it well; but since He sends you the infirmities you suffer, He wills all the privations and afflictions which follow from them.

All this is very good (it will still be said), but it is the occasion of such great humiliations: people look upon you with an evil eye in a house; they treat you with coldness and contempt; they grow tired at last of helping and waiting on you. Let them be as charitable as you please, in the case of an obstinate illness, if the discomforts attending it are of long duration, particular!' Where there is nothing very noteworthy about them, many of your wants will often remain unsupplied. Will you then complain that Heaven bestows too many favours upon you? If your crosses are so great, you are all the more blessed in the sight of God. And here I must not omit to tell you that God sometimes allows persons of great virtue to be so sensitively alive to their pains that, unless you were gifted with great discernment, you might think them very impatient, although in the depth of their soul they are admirably resigned to the Divine Will. The sufferings of St. Catherine of Genoa made her at times rend the air with her cries, as we learn from the history of her life. I have myself known persons of extraordinary virtue with whom the same thing occurred. This serves to humble them, and to conceal virtues which would ravish us with their beauty if they were displayed before our eyes. Certainly that mirror of patience, the Blessed Henry Suso, wept and cried aloud, and that sometimes in the very streets, in the excess of his sufferings. Persons who give way to impatience must not make this an excuse for their own want of resignation; but such as are truly resigned may take comfort from these examples, if the inferior portion of their soul is sensibly affected, and that even to tears: this does not prevent their will being entirely conformed to the Will of God.

CHAPTER V.

THE LOSS OF HONOR.

Let a man do what he will in the way of austerities, alms deeds, catechizing, preaching, prayers, if he does not arrive at the contempt of honor he will never attain to a perfect union with our Lord; for it was what He most loved and held dearest in this world, and was the state in which He was born and died. Strange, that we would have none of that which a Man-God was always seeking: or, if we are willing to have it, we soon weary of what He loved to the very last moment of His divine life. What shall we say, then, of the human prudence of some spiritual persons, who hold and declare that, in order to do good, it is necessary to enjoy credit and reputation among men? That great Saint, Teresa, regards this maxim, not only as indefensible, but as most pernicious. Let me repeat what was said elsewhere: Are we wiser than Eternal Wisdom, in discovering more efficient ways of doing good than those which He Himself selected? O my soul, let us fix our eyes on that perfect pattern, and never divert them from it. Let us consider that such was His extreme abhorrence of worldly honour that at His birth He appears in a miserable stable, between two brute beasts, on a little straw. Is not this a strangely abject "state for the King of kings to be born in? Not long after He flies ingloriously before His persecutors; He passes His childhood in a foreign land, amid great poverty; then He leads a hidden life in the workshop of a poor carpenter, even till He has attained the age of thirty years. O You wretched point of honour, how are You trodden under foot by the God of all glory! How far removed are Your ways, O my God, from the ways of men! Is it possible that the holy family of Jesus, Mary, and Joseph —a family of no distinction, possessing none of the goods of this life, without attendant or servant—the family of a poor artisan known to nobody—is destined to be at the head of all the Blessed in everlasting glory? It is true that the Adorable Jesus appears in public during three years and more; but alas! It is only to see Himself loaded with indignities and satiated with outrages. If His preaching creates a sensation, there will be found persons to make a mock of it, and even among His own kinsmen there will be some who will look upon Him as one bereft of His senses, and will desire to lay hold on Him as a madman.

Yet the people are divided in opinion; some saying that He was a good man, and others maintaining that He was a deceiver and a hypocrite. Perhaps, amongst all this diversity of opinion, some would suspend their judgment, saying that it would be well to wait and see what would happen. O Eternal Father, will You not justify the innocence of Your Well Beloved Son? No, the heavens are not so far removed from the earth as are the ways of God from those of men. And now, let us consider what these persons are doing who thus suspend their judgment, and who to human eyes appear the most judicious, saying that it was best not to be in a hurry: they are in fact putting this Divine Saviour on His trial; and, at first sight, does it not appear that His affairs could not be proceeding better? Sooner or later, people say, innocence is recognized; without a doubt, the man who is guiltless of the slightest fault will be acquitted; and how should it be otherwise 1 Behold Him, then, seized and accused. O Infinite Goodness, O Mercy, O Exceeding Charity! You permit many witnesses to testify against You: true, they are false witnesses; still they are witnesses. This gracious Saviour is accused of crimes against God, against men, and against Himself, of crimes the most atrocious: namely, of high treason against God and man, the assumption of Divinity, and the usurpation of earthly sovereignty. The cry is that He is a seducer of the people, a disturber of the public peace; that He is a drunkard, and in secret league with devils; yea, that he is Himself possessed. He is led before the ecclesiastical tribunal: doubtless the pontiffs and the priests will favour His innocence; the doctors of the law will not allow themselves to be duped. Alas! These are the very men who will be the most eager to condemn Him, while the high priest, by rending his garments, gives evident proof of the horror with which he regards Him. He is brought before the governor of the province, before King Herod; and everywhere He is condemned. What greater ignominy can there be than this, for the world did not fail to say, " See, he is condemned by pontiffs, by kings, and other judges; he is declared guilty in every kind of court, ecclesiastical and secular; his guilt has been proved by the testimony of witnesses. It has been made clearly manifest that all the sanctity which this man displayed was nothing but hypocrisy, and his miracles mere delusion: good reason was there for saying that he was a deceiver, a seducer of the people, who allowed themselves to be led away by this fellow? Everything is now brought to light, he has been arraigned, and has been tried, and sentence has been pronounced upon him."

What helped greatly also to lend credit to these assertions was the conduct of His disciples. Observe (people said), it is not only his adversaries who take against him; one of his own disciples delivered him up to our chief priests: sure sign that he knew the real character of the man. The one who appeared the most zealous among them judged his life to be so disgraceful that he did not even dare admit to a simple maidservant that he was acquainted with him, and preferred perjuring himself to confessing that he was one of his followers. The others all abandoned him: a pretty clear proof of the truth of the charges brought against him. True, there are three or four weak women who still adhere to him; but it is just your women who let themselves be carried away by passion, instead of following the dictates of right reason. Anyhow, he must be a strange sort of personage, seeing that robbers and murderers are preferred before him, and it is God-fearing people who take measures against him: people who are actively engaged in works of mercy, begging for a prisoner's release, and so religious that they would not transgress the law by entering the governor's hall, because, by so doing, they would have contracted a legal defilement. To all this it was added that God, who is the protector of the innocent, had Himself abandoned him, although he had called upon Him with a loud voice; so that, in the face of so many things, it was no longer possible to doubt his impostures: in fine, that he had died upon a Cross, an accursed death—so declared, not only in the opinion of the vulgar, but on the authority of the Sacred Scriptures. Such, O human prudence, is the conduct of a God-Man. Behold, ye wise spiritual men, how a God applied Himself to work the greatest good that ever was wrought.

But at least (someone will say) He did not wish to be accused or to be suspected in the matter of purity. I reply, It is sufficient that the Virgin of virgins, His immaculate Mother, should have been suspected of adultery, to show that we must be ready to suffer in our honour in all sorts of ways. Accordingly, this Divine Master, to anticipate these objections, after saying to His disciples, " Blessed are ye when they shall revile you," adds—not without design — and when they " shall speak all that is evil against you " (Matt. 5:11). Do you see how He makes no exception and, in fact, how many of His saints have been maligned in the matter of purity!

"Is it possible," exclaimed St. Teresa, " that I should desire, O my God, that men should have a good opinion of me, when they have spoken so much evil of Thee?" This is why the Apostle protests (Gal. 6:14) that the world is crucified to him, and that he is crucified to the world: that is to say, the world and its honour were as much objects of abhorrence to him as the sight of a man fastened to an infamous gibbet is to a passer-by; and, on the other hand, he was himself an object of abhorrence to the world, seeing as it did that he loved what it detested, namely, contempt and ignominy; for which reason also this great Apostle declares (1 Cor. 4:10) that he was looked upon as a fool and a madman. Oh, what good reason had St. Ignatius, the founder of the Company of Jesus, to say to his children, who are destined to accomplish such great things in their several offices, that every state in which we are mocked and despised by men, and even held to be wicked and mad, is a state that is very precious in the spiritual life. " I would wish," says the saint I have just quoted, " that we should study to do penance by the love of contempt and calumnies: for this, bodily strength is not required."

CHAPTER VI.

PERSECUTIONS ON THE PART OF MEN.

It is an undoubted truth, for we have it from Truth Itself (2 Tim. 3:12), that " all that will live godly in Christ Jesus shall suffer persecution." The servant is not greater than his lord. If the world cruelly persecuted its Sovereign, the Lord of all, it will not spare His disciples. How could the world fail to make war on those who are opposed to it, seeing that it ill-treats in so pitiless a manner all who are most zealous in maintaining His cause? This is why it has been declared by the Holy Spirit (Ecclus. 2:1), that he who would dispose himself for the service of God "must prepare his soul for temptation."

Heaven having, by an extraordinary favour of love, given to St. Elizabeth of Hungary—I am writing this on the feast day of that admirable servant of God— the great St. John the Evangelist for her guide and director, that amiable saint, so beloved of Jesus and Mary, foretold to her that she would never lack crosses. It is the great grace vouchsafed to all the friends of our Saviour, who, amid the numerous sufferings that befall them, have always to suffer much from the world. If a man withdraws from its society, in order to give himself to more earnest thought of his salvation, it inveighs against his churlish humor. If his conversation is of a grave and serious cast, it says that his devotion is calculated to deter and repel people, and that such a way of acting is enough to inspire disgust for the service of God. If he is of a cheerful and genial disposition, this is at once made the subject of raillery, men saying that your pious folk can enjoy themselves as well as others, and that it is easy to be devout after that sort of fashion. If he meet with any untoward accident in his affairs, or if he incur a loss of goods, immediately the blame is laid on his piety: people accuse him of not having given the needful attention to household duties, although this is entirely false, and everything had been done that could have been done. If persons have an unamiable nature, and fall into some fault, devotion is made to answer for it all, as says the great St. Francis de Sales. In short the whole life of those who serve God is narrowly scrutinized, little heed being given to the injustice committed in the judgments that are passed.

In truth it must be allowed that there are persons who are sorely tried, and who seem to live only to be a butt for contradiction. The wound which tongues inflict by backbiting, calumnies, scoffing, and a thousand offensive speeches is one of those which is most keenly felt. If a man falls into some actual fault, you would say that to publish it abroad was to render great glory to God. If it is a fault of little consequence, the human mind is ingenious in finding means to make it seem important, and sometimes these slight faults will give occasion to a violent persecution. It is related in the Life of that holy man, Father John of the Cross,1 that after all the formal inquiries that were made into his conduct, the articles drawn up against him, granting they had been true, consisted only of venial sins. And yet what a clamor and excitement did not this information create! If a man's good actions are too patent to be denied, then he is accused of hypocrisy, his peculiar gifts are attributed to the devil, and his whole life is declared to be nothing but deception and fraud. If he speaks unaffectedly of some mercy vouchsafed by our Lord, people cry out at his want of humility. If he keeps silence amidst the charges heaped upon him, it is taken as a proof of his guilt: a man is bound in conscience, they will say, to vindicate himself, and that, too, where the honor of God is concerned. If he opens his mouth, saints, they will say, never spoke a word; and if he deems that on certain occasions he ought to give expression to his thoughts, it is imputed to pride. You would say that the minds of men were filled with nothing but hostility to these persons. Those who ill-treat them are commended, and people actually think that they ought to be thankful to those who injure them most. All is good in others, all is bad in them. Here is what the Recluse of Flanders says, in her excellent book on The Ruin of Self-love:

" If people perceive some natural emotion in which there is nothing whatever sinful, they will make great vices out of it, and will say, ' Look at your saintly personage!' And this is true, not only of worldly people, but even of the most spiritual, and sometimes of the person's own confessor, who hardly knows what to think of his penitent. There is no calumny which is not launched against him, and owing to the false reports which are disseminated by worthy people, who think that in doing so they are acting well, a person who before was held in honour and credit, and esteemed by all that was best and most virtuous, behold! He is become the object of scorn and contempt, and is abandoned by everyone; and, what is worse, it appears as if the spirits, and even God Himself, were leagued together to heap suffering upon him."

Before concluding this little work, I will, by God's help, point out to you an illustrious instance of this in the person of St. Teresa, referring the reader who would wish to know

93

more on the subject to my book on The Servitude of the
Admirable Mother of God, where I have brought together
a number of examples. Here it is sufficient to say that
the great servant of God, Father Baltasar Alvarez, of the
Company of Jesus, confessor of the Saint whom I have just
mentioned, and to whom it was revealed that there was no
one in the world who surpassed him in perfection, had to
suffer cruelly from men, and even from some of his own
Company. False witness was given against him; he was
charged with a serious offence in a General Congregation
of his Society, and was made responsible for the faults of
his followers, who had used erroneous language on the
subject of prayer. It is an injustice of which men are apt to
be guilty, to attribute to directors the failings of those who
are under their direction. St. Teresa declares that he had
no little to go through on account of the judgments passed
against herself. Everything was laid at his door.

But, after all these carpings at individuals, people come
next to canvassing the state itself. Observe what St. Teresa
says in the second chapter of The Way of Perfection: "Such
things as these are often said to us"—she is speaking of
mental prayer—"' This way is full of peril; it was the ruin
of such a person, another got involved in error; a third, who
prayed a great deal, fell away altogether; this is injurious to
the practice of virtue, that is not good for women, and the
less so because they are liable to delusions; they had better
go spin: the Pater and Ave are quite enough.'"

Amid all these persecutions, never forget that all creatures
are nothing before God, and therefore that you ought
not to trouble yourself at being assailed by that which is
nothing. Ah, poor soul, how disturbed you are! Yet why
distress yourself about nothing? Compose your mind a
little, recollect yourself: it is nothing. Oh, how clearly will

you discern this truth at the moment of death! Courage!
The world soon passes away, and sooner for you than
you think. After death, what harm will the contradiction
of tongues, the contempt of men, the humiliating loss of
honour do you? What! All creatures together are nothing
before God; their words, then, are less than nothing. Truly,
is not this a folly? Whatever lights you may have received,
whether by infused and supernatural illumination or by
acquired knowledge—were you the most learned person in
the world—if you have not perfectly mastered this science
of nothingness, you are far removed from the kingdom of
God. But this science must be reduced to practice; and it is
easy to prove whether it be so: if you still disquiet yourself
with the thought of what people will say of this or that, it
is an infallible sign that you do not possess it. Listen, O
would be spiritual man: You are still engulfed in darkness,
if You are disturbed about the opinion of men. God Alone,
God Alone, God Alone is sufficient. Test Yourself by this
touchstone.

Never, therefore, expect any great things from people
who are so cautious of their honor and reputation, and so
sensitive to what is thought or said about them. Observe,
moreover, the uselessness of all the trouble they take: for
these persons who are so touchy on a point of honour,
who, from policy, try to win all hearts, and who never
neglect any means of pleasing everybody, with all their
efforts—I am speaking even of those who are reckoned
the most complaisant of human beings, and of whom it
is said that they are liked by one and all—these persons
none the less receive secret cuts, which wound them to the
quick, and give them besides ample matter for reflection.
How much meanness, and not infrequently sins, must these
persons be habitually guilty of, in order to avoid offending
people! How many treasons against conscience! How

many connivances at vice, allowing it to go unpunished! How many malversations in their employments! How many frightful crimes in the presentation or collation of benefices! What toleration of irregularities in individuals and in communities!

Hold it, then, as a maxim, never to do anything for the sake of pleasing men, and never to omit doing anything for fear of displeasing them. Quit the creature, and look to God Alone. There are certain indifferent things which ought to be given up, after the example of the great Apostle, when they excite a clamor and scandalize the weak. But we are bound to persevere in doing good, in spite of the contradiction of tongues, following the example of the Son of God, who continued to eat with publicans and sinners, that thence He might take occasion to draw them away from their vices, leaving the Scribes and Pharisees, who took scandal and murmured greatly thereat, to say what they pleased. He who should act otherwise would rob God of a great glory which accrues to Him from a number of excellent actions; and the devil would have no difficulty in preventing a very large amount of good, since it is easy for him to raise evil reports and scandals in order to bring it to naught. That great servant of God of whom I have spoken, Baltasar Alvarez, when suffering much, as has been said, on account of St. Teresa—people loudly complaining of her being under his direction— sent her word that he would never give her up, for all these outcries and evil surmisings. He was a man who looked to God Alone. The Saint was firmly convinced that we ought to hold in contempt all the talk of men regarding the practice of virtues: this is why she speaks in this wise: " If people say that it is not well to go so often to Communion—why then we go only the more frequently; if they say there is danger in (mental) prayer, the servant of God endeavors to show what great profit there is in such prayer." She said moreover, " Do not let yourself be led away by any one, be he who he may, who would show you any other path save that of prayer. If anyone tell you there is danger in it, look upon him as being himself a dangerous man. Avoid him: be sure and never forget this. To say that the way of prayer is perilous —this is what God never permits. It is one of the devil's devices to excite such fears. Consider, on the other hand, the great blindness of the world, which does not see the thousands of souls that are lost for lack of prayer; while, if any one meets with a fall on this road, then would it fain fill all hearts with dread. For myself, I have never noted any snare of the devil more pernicious than this."

I will conclude this chapter with those words of Scripture (James 4:4): " Know you not that the friendship of this world is the enemy of God?" This it is that makes the great St. Paul say (Gal. 1:10), " If I pleased men, I should not be the servant of Jesus Christ." I leave you to ponder these truths at your leisure; you will then see whether we need care for the friendship of men, or take pains to please them.

CHAPTER VII.

CONTRADICTIONS ON THE PART OF THE GOOD.

They who belong to Jesus Christ and His most holy Mother suffer from men in various ways. Some persecute them through envy, jealousy, or revenge; because their good life is opposed to their own practice; because they cannot endure the splendor of their fervent charity; because the ardor of their zeal is directed to the destruction of their own corrupted morals, to their reformation, and the establishment of a holy discipline. Others persecute them, thinking to do God service, and acting with good and upright intentions. Now among these latter there are some who harass good people without committing any sin; God permitting them to have just ground for doing so. Father Luis de Ponte, of the Company of Jesus, in his Life of Father Baltasar Alvarez, adduces on this subject the example of the glorious St. Joseph, who suspected the most holy Virgin of criminal conduct without any fault on his part, because he perceived that she was pregnant, and could not possibly know of the conception of the Eternal Word in her womb by the operation of the Holy Ghost.

It is true that the number of these persons is very small, for the corruption of nature, self-love, and the secret motives of self-interest are actively at work, almost everywhere. Corrupt nature, then, often mixes itself up with the best intentions; for either we take things up too warmly, or push them too far, or are too eager to attain our purposes, or are afraid of appearing to have been mistaken. Or, again, we allow ourselves to be easily prejudiced, being too ready to listen to accusations, letting our minds be pre-occupied and our memory engrossed with the faults that are alleged, without giving sufficient time to weigh the reasons on the opposite side. Or we allow too much scope for the operation of the devil, who, desiring on such occasions to get possession of the imagination, magnifies the appearances of things, and stirs and excites the passions; so that we are not fairly disposed to feel the force of the true reasons, to which indeed we scarcely listen. We have a signal example of this in the person of one of the superiors of the Venerable Father John of the Cross, who persisted in treating the servant of God in the harshest manner, even going so far as to dislike any one visiting him: and, in fact, we find it recorded that a devil had got possession of this man's imagination, so that nothing that could possibly be said to the saint's advantage had the slightest effect upon him, but his mind continued to be filled with anger and bitterness. Now these persons, with all their good intentions, are nevertheless culpable; and, after having served as God's instruments in purifying and sanctifying His holiest servants, they are themselves chastised, either in this world, or in the other life, in Purgatory, by great sufferings, as we learn from the Lives of the Saints. True it is that these persons would not wish to act in bad faith, but their fault is in allowing themselves to be deceived, either for such reasons as I have mentioned or for others. In fine, it is a serious matter to make the servants of God suffer, whatever good intentions we may have, and the devil makes use of this for his own purposes.

The purpose of the All-Good God in thus trying His servants is the promotion of His own glory and the sanctification of their souls; and He establishes His kingdom in an admirable manner by means of the hardships and persecutions which they undergo: thus He accomplishes His greatest designs by the way of the Cross, a way hidden from the wisdom of men, who cannot persuade themselves that humiliations and abasements are profitable means for doing good. For what apparent ground is there for supposing that a man should succeed the better in his Apostolic functions because he is repulsed, abandoned, calumniated, and otherwise made to suffer? Does it not seem that such a person stands in need of a high reputation, and of the esteem and friendship of creatures'! Yet, if you cast your eyes on the Adorable Jesus, the holy Apostles who converted the world, the greatest saints who have been the most signal instruments of Divine Providence, you will see them accomplish all the great designs of God under the heavy weight of every kind of cross.

This is why God permits them to be tried, not only by the wicked, but also by the good. It were little to suffer at the hands of those whose testimony against us is not calculated to produce the fullest impression on men's minds; it is fitting that we should suffer at the hands of persons of known probity, whose judgment cannot easily be set aside. Such were they who persecuted St. Teresa: their authority was so great and their virtues so deservedly acknowledged, that not to credit them would have been a high offence, as is remarked by the prelate who wrote the Life of that saint. Accordingly the holy Father Peter of Alcantara observes that the persecution she had to endure from good people was one of the severest trials she went through. " The stings of honey-bees," said our Lord, in reference to this subject, to a holy superioress, " are far more painful than those of other insects." People do not fail to say that the charges are proved, because good men have passed their condemnation on the accused. They believe that persons like these, who are no novices in the matter of virtue, and are very enlightened, cannot be deceived; and even when passion has had its influence, they cannot be persuaded that it is so. Consequently they acquiesce in the condemnation of persons, without hesitation or the smallest remorse of conscience; and hence results that thorough abasement of these sorely tried souls which God designs to effect by these ways of His, and which would not be brought about if the wicked alone were numbered among their adversaries.

The devil, on the other hand, has many other purposes in these contradictions, using them to prevent a thousand good things which might be accomplished by means of God's servants thus persecuted; discrediting or, at least, throwing suspicion on their conduct, in order that no confidence may be reposed in them, seeing as he does that God vouchsafes them extraordinary graces in the employments they undertake. Sometimes he even transforms himself into an angel of light, and appearing to persons, gives them counsels conformable with his designs, in order to deter souls from having recourse to God's servants; coloring things with specious pretexts of the glory of God and the purity of consciences; and, if it happens that these illusions are taken for divine revelations, he carries matters to incredible lengths, because those who have been deceived by them are persuaded that they are acting in obedience to God's commands. Let good people beware of seconding the designs of this infernal spirit; and let them learn once for all that, although we are not aware of it, we often favour his schemes, even with very good intentions, which he is not slow to profit by, as I have frequently said.

CHAPTER VIII.

ABANDONMENT BY CREATURES, AND PARTICULARLY BY FRIENDS.

We often complain of what ought to be a subject of joy to us; and when we think ourselves most miserable, then it is that we are most happy. This truth is clearly evident to those who avail themselves of the lights of faith, with respect to this abandonment by creatures and especially by friends. Unquestionably the being forsaken by friends and relatives, or by persons who are under great obligations to us, is one of those things to which we are most painfully sensitive. The Blessed Henry Suso, having been accused by a wretched woman of being the father of a child, which she brought to him and left in his hands, sought consolation from some of his spiritual friends, but found himself harshly repulsed: they refused even to speak to him. This is what very commonly happens: people are shy of consorting with those who are suffering under humiliations. Now the holy man acknowledged that this was a blow which he felt very keenly; and does not the Prophet, speaking in the person of our gracious Saviour, declare (Ps. 54:5, 13—15) that the being abandoned by friends was a grievous affliction and an exceeding great sorrow to him?

Yet the Christian, who is a man of grace—whose life is therefore supernatural—finds inestimable blessings in the severest privations of nature. To say all in one word—he finds God, Where creatures are no longer, there God Alone is to be found. O sweet, O lovely truths, which constitute the Paradise of souls. Ah, if men did but know you! The Spirit of love—we read in the Life of St. Catherine of Genoa—took from her all her friends, and those spiritual persons from whom she received consolation, and she remained solitary and forsaken, as well interiorly as exteriorly; He deprived her even of her confessor. This was because God wished to make of her a creature all divine: and in fact this saint was incomparable for pure love of God Alone. St. Paul no longer lived; it was Jesus alone who lived in that Apostolic man;1 but he was exalted to so glorious a possession by extreme privations. O my God, how wonderful are the dealings of Providence! The great Apostle found himself forsaken by the Galatians; he had even come to be regarded as their enemy, because he had freely told them the truth: he found himself rejected by the very people respecting whom he had used such marvelous language in speaking (4:14—15) of the friendship they had shown him: how they had received him as an angel of God, even as Christ Jesus; and, so to say,—these are the Apostle's own words,—would have plucked out their own eyes, and given them to him, if he had needed them. Does he not declare in the Second Epistle to Timothy (4:16) that he found himself forsaken by all? But at the same time he adds (v. 17) that the Lord stood by him: so true it is that where creatures fail us, there we find God.

But what has there ever been like to the Sacred Humanity of the Adorable Jesus, which was united hypostatically to the Divine Word, so that we say with truth that Jesus is God and yet, wonderful to relate, no one was ever abandoned as He was. He is betrayed by one of His disciples; the chief of His Apostles denies Him; all forsake Him; the angels leave Him to the cruelty of His enemies; He parts with His holy Mother, quitting her at the foot of the Cross; the Holy Spirit leads Him to the sacrifice, as the Apostle teaches (Heb. 9:14); the Eternal Father abandons Him; yea, He abandons Himself: so that His people, His creatures, heaven and earth, and, as an excellent writer observes, His Father, His Mother, the Holy Spirit, and Jesus Himself combine together to afflict Jesus. All powers—divine, celestial, human, and infernal—join in tormenting Him.

These considerations, if the soul be penetrated, even but a little, therewith, excite more desire than fear of being abandoned by creatures. No, no; let nature shrink as it will, let the human mind reason as much as it pleases, this spectacle of a God-Man thus forsaken inspires an incredible longing for every kind of dereliction. How is it possible, after this, not to be fired with a holy passion and languish with love for these dear abandonments? What a blessedness to have some share in them! How happy we ought to esteem ourselves! What lot can be compared with that which gives us admission into states through which the King of heaven and earth has passed! Only the resolution I have taken to give no more than a short abridgment of this subject in the present work restrains me: there is matter enough here to occupy my pen for the remainder of my life.

O welcome, happy, joyful news, when word is brought us that we are being deserted by everyone, even by those of whom we should never have believed it possible! Go, says the soul,—go, ye creatures; I am well content you should depart, for your departure is to me the sweet approach of the Creator. Ah! What a blessed exchange! God instead of the creature! Let me repeat it: God instead of the creature! O my soul, what more fatal delusion than to seek for consolation in created being! Deceitful consolations, ye are vast and veritable desolations. This is what happens: we act pretty much like those who feel themselves slipping down a precipice; they catch at everything they can to prevent their falling; if there is anything within reach on which they can lay fast hold, to that they will cling. Alas! This is what those cowardly creatures do who, being attracted and invited to the glorious losing of themselves in the abyss of God's Being by the union of His grace, grasp at whatever comes to hand, and will not let themselves sink into the abyss so long as they can find anything to hold by. O divine abyss, O beloved abyss, may my poor soul lose itself in You, never more to find itself.

O wonderful and dread necessity—to leave all in order to find all! The Apostles after the Resurrection loved Jesus, their good Master, not only as Man, but as the Son of God: yet, because they loved Him also for their own consolation and satisfaction, it was expedient that He should withdraw from them, even as He had been constrained to tell them (John 16:7). Learn, hence, O souls who are afflicted with interior abandonments, that it is profitable thus to suffer. Magdalen turns her back upon the angels who address her, although she might have received from them unspeakable consolations: for true it is that angels and saints are but means by which to go to the Creator, and that we must leave them when they would distract our minds from Him; as sometimes happens to exalted souls when they are actually engaged in the prayer of union. But much

more than this: we must even die to Jesus, in the sense
He has indicated, in order to live only to Jesus, for Jesus,
and by Jesus. This was the practice of the great St. Paul,
who protested (2 Cor. 5:16) that he knew Jesus no longer
according to the flesh, that is, so far as might gratify the
love of self. We must fix our eyes upon His Godhead, for
this Divine Saviour Himself could not endure to be called "
good " when regarded only as a prophet or a saint. " Good
Master," one said to Him (Mark 10:17): what words could
have seemed more fitting? Nevertheless He will not accept
them. For immediately He replies (v. 18), "None is good
but One—God." Let us, then, ever say, God Alone, God
Alone, God Alone.

PRAYER TO THE MOST HOLY VIRGIN, CONSOLER OF THE AFFLICTED.

Holy Virgin, rightly do Christians everywhere invoke You
as Our Lady of Consolation. Most fitly does the Church
sing that You are the consoler of the afflicted, for who
can look with an eye of faith on all that passed during the
course of Your holy life, so full of crosses, without being
mightily consoled? That You are the Mother of God we
cannot doubt without sin, and yet we know that He gave
You, as Your portion in this world, poverty, contempt, and
sorrow; and therefore are we most certainly assured that
these sufferings are the richest gifts of Heaven. How, then,
can we fail to be consoled, and abound with joy, at seeing
ourselves honoured with such favours? Holy Virgin, may
these truths never pass from before our eyes, and may the
love of You abide ever in our hearts, that we may make a
holy use of them. Amen.

PART III.

INTERIOR TRIALS.

CHAPTER I.

OF INTERIOR SUFFERINGS; AND FIRST OF
TEMPTATIONS TO UNBELIEF AND BLASPHEMY.

A Certain author has well said that, as the interior
crosses of Christians are an expression and an imitation
of the interior crosses of Jesus Christ, and as this life of
crucifixion through sufferings that are not visible represents
the hidden life of a God-Man, wherein are comprehended
the most astounding of His mysteries, so also they who
bear these crosses are the most striking likenesses of this
Divine Saviour. Other martyrs have angels and men for
their spectators; these have God alone for their witness: this
it is that renders these states especially holy, because they
shut us out from the sympathy of creatures, who have but
little pity or praise to bestow on what they neither see nor
understand. And yet these sufferings far surpass all exterior
pains, which are easy crosses when the mind is at rest. This
made St. Teresa say that the labours of contemplatives were
incomparably more severe than those of the active life.

In commencing to treat of these it is well to descend to
details, and in the first place to speak of the sufferings
which proceed from temptations against faith. They who
have had some experience of this kind of trial will confess
that it is the hardest and most terrible of all. It is when
suffering under this ordeal that a soul may take to itself
those words of the prophet (Lam. 3:9): " He has shut
up my ways with square stones "; for all its avenues are
closed to consolation. In other trials there remains at least

one consolation, which is the thought of God; I mean the belief that there is a God: for as to the actual conscious remembrance of Him, this is often taken away in many other temptations. But here the doubt is added whether there be a God. Whence, then, can we look for consolation? From earth? Alas! That cannot be. From Heaven? It seems to have vanished altogether. From this present life? But it is precisely there we find our pains. From the other life? There seems to be none. Verily, this trial is distressing beyond measure.

Nevertheless souls ought not to be cast down by these crosses. They should remember that the All- Good God has laid them on many of His saints. A great number of the elect have trodden this way. In our own time we have seen a Mother de Chantal, so eminent for her virtues, weeping bitterly and saying that she beheld herself without faith, without hope, without charity. We have seen a holy General of a reformed Order so tormented with this temptation— albeit one who by his counsels and spiritual writings was the consoler of all who were tempted, being himself a great master of the interior life—so tormented, I say, that he was constrained to cry aloud, " I believe, I believe," inquiring of the religious around him if they had heard him pronounce those words.

What, then, ought we to do when we are thus afflicted, except carefully to beware of reasoning on the subject, not allowing ourselves to give in to an artifice of the evil spirit, who suggests that the way to free ourselves from this temptation is to look about for arguments. Experience sufficiently shows that it is the means of perplexing ourselves still more. But I say to you further, in a case like this avoid contending with the devil. If once you engage in argument with this wily spirit, you are caught in the snare, and your perdition is all but assured. It is related that when a certain learned man was on his deathbed, the devil, taking human shape, came to him under the appearance of a distinguished theologian, as though to pay him a visit of civility, and that, being led to reason with the disguised demon on matters of faith, the dying man was near incurring the loss of his soul. Well was it for him that he cast his eyes on an image of the holy Virgin which was near his bed; for this look of love put the enemy to flight, and but for the succor of the Mother of Mercy it would have been all over with him. St. Francis de Sales declared that without extraordinary assistance from Heaven, he would have succumbed to a very subtle temptation against the Most Holy Sacrament of the Altar; a temptation so fraught with peril, that this great bishop, sensible of its dangerous character, would never mention what it was.

All heresies come simply from the liberty people take of examining into the truths of religion, relying on their own lights, their own reasoning, the interpretations they put on Scripture, on Councils, or on the decisions of Sovereign Pontiffs, contrary to the doctrine of the great Apostle, who clearly teaches(2 Cor. 10:5) that we must " bring the understanding into captivity to the obedience of faith." For what does he mean by this " captivity" of the understanding, unless it be that we must keep it restrained and bound under the obedience of faith, believing simply what God has revealed either immediately or by His Church, subjecting our mind to the decisions of Councils and of Sovereign Pontiffs, whom the Son of God has commissioned to confirm their brethren in the faith? We ought to learn wisdom from the experience of so many centuries, which teach us that heretics have never wanted plausible reasons, ingenious and seemingly strong; making use of Scripture, which they constantly quote, as well as of the authority of the Fathers; publishing fine works which captivate by the charm of their style and the beauty of their eloquence: and many of them even winning hearts by the example of an austere and edifying life and contempt of the world. But because they have been wanting in a sincere submission to the head of the Church and to its Councils, they have miserably gone astray, together with those who followed them. Many 'kingdoms have lost the faith in this manner. O blessed they, who, obeying in simplicity the Pope and the Church, have remained faithful to the true religion! The Lutherans and Calvinists of the last century cried out that the Pope was in error, and that they desired a General Council; but afterwards, seeing themselves condemned also by the Council, they said that it was not a legitimate one, on account of the Pope's intrigues; and, in saying these things, they awfully deceived themselves, together with all their adherents, whom they involved with themselves in, everlasting damnation. Those who were living at that time and who adhered to Sovereign Pontiffs and to Councils, preserved the faith for themselves and their posterity; and if we live in a Catholic country, we owe it to their obedience.

The great remedy, then, in these temptations is that which St. Francis de Sales prescribed: to take to flight by the gate of the will, leaving that of the reasoning spirit. This is a case in which the counsel of the masters of the spiritual life ought to be followed, who so strongly recommend abstraction. Then it is that we ought to have recourse to it, even during the time of prayer, keeping ourselves in a state of complete abstraction by a direct act, avoiding all voluntary reflections: I say voluntary, for it is impossible to prevent a thousand thoughts flowing in from all sides; only we must let them pass without dwelling on them, at least with deliberate intention. Of this I have treated more largely in my book On the Reign of God in Mental Prayer.

But what are persons doing (someone will say) during such a state of abstraction? They are making a number of excellent acts, as we have shown in the book above cited, and particularly that of faith, which is so much the more pure and safe as it is less self- conscious, and cannot be combated by the devil, which vexes him much: this is why he neglects nothing by which to make us descend to sensible operations, in order that he may have the opportunity of contending with the soul, for he can do nothing against it so long as it is withdrawn into the fortress of its inmost centre.

But how is it possible for me to produce acts of faith, when I am deprived of it? One will say who is suffering under this trial. " I cannot make any acts," said the holy Mother de Chantal: " it is to me a very martyrdom to see everyone enjoying the benefit of faith and myself deprived of it." " This is to deceive oneself," replies a great prelate; " we are not deprived of the act of faith, although it seems so to us, because we do not perceive it. Under a large heap of hot cinders there is still a live coal, and all the more glowing because it is covered up; fire enclosed in a furnace being much more intense than that which is open to the air. And, in fact, faith must be very lively to preserve the soul in the fear of God amidst all this confusion. Ah! You complain of no longer having faith; and it is faith which makes you complain in this wise. If you no longer had faith, why should you fear sin and temptation? He who is really without faith, like the atheists, abandons himself to all sorts of crimes. Why do you behave with reverence in presence of the Blessed Sacrament, why do you go to confession, unless you believe in these sacraments? It is as true, then, that you have faith, as it is certain that you are not sensible of it."

In regard to temptations to blasphemy, they are not so dangerous; they frighten more than they hurt us, by the horror they inspire. Remember, that even should all the blasphemies of hell pass through your mind, you would be none the less pleasing in the sight of God. Learn once for all that the most accursed thoughts do not make us criminals; but only a perfect and entire consent of the will. Do not disquiet yourself; your will, your heart, does not freely take part in these horrible blasphemies, any more than in attacks on your faith. The temptation is so urgent, and the poor mind is so oppressed, that we think we consent when we resist. Try to remain as tranquil as you can, and, above all, avoid all sadness and voluntary disquietude.

" O my dear Theophilus," exclaims the illustrious prelate De Belley, in his Spiritual Conflict, " if you did but know the gift of God! These temptations which you take for torrents devastating your faith, are to me so many honourable tokens of your fidelity; and such, I am persuaded, will be the judgment of those who have any experience in this spiritual encounter or conflict. You execrate it, and I bless it; and, should I wish to denounce it, I should have no more power to do so than had Balaam to hurl his curses on the army of Israel. The devil, that shameless one, had the audacity to say to the Son of God that he would give Him kingdoms if He would fall done and adore him. If such ideas, then, pass through your mind, can you be surprised? Do you suppose that he stands more in awe of the disciple than of the Master?"

I will conclude this chapter with some sentiments of St. Teresa. " I declare," she said, " that the more difficulty I experience in conceiving a mystery of the faith, the stronger inclination I have to believe it, and the more devotion I feel for it. My mind finds instant satisfaction in any difficulty, when I consider with myself that God can act in a manner I do not understand, and without its being necessary to make me comprehend it or appreciate it. I feel myself so strong that I seem as if I could do battle with all the Lutherans for the least ceremony of the Church." This great saint, when on her death-bed, declared that her consolation was to die " a daughter of the Church"; to which the holy Sister Mary of the Incarnation added, " and a daughter of the Blessed Virgin." Let not souls marvel if they are not sensible of having inclinations and thoughts such as these: as has been said, let them abide in the faith which is hidden in their inmost depth, and no longer disquiet themselves about anything.

CHAPTER II.

TEMPTATIONS TO DREAD OF REPROBATION, DESPONDENCY, AND DESPAIR.

St. Teresa, in the first chapter of the Sixth Chamber of the Interior Castle, writes that the devil makes the soul think that it is rejected by God. She might say this of her own experience, having—to use the words of the Bishop who wrote her Life—been stricken by Heaven, as if God had turned His back upon her. One of her nuns in the Convent of Alva was tormented for seven years by devils, who persuaded her that she was lost beyond recovery. "It seems to me," said St. Catherine of Genoa, "that I am utterly deprived of the aid of God; at least, I have no conscious experience of it." In our own days the great St. Francis de Sales was assailed with these temptations; nor would it be possible to enumerate the many holy souls who have been thus cruelly afflicted.

And yet, beyond all doubt, God truly wills our salvation. Nay, further, He wills it more than we will it ourselves; and He has done more to save us than we shall ever do, or, indeed, can do: this it is which is so infinitely consoling. True, we love ourselves, we are attached beyond conception to whatever affects ourselves or our own interests; but it is even more indubitable that God has a greater love for us, and a greater desire of our good than we can have ourselves. Let anyone who doubts it cast his eyes on His self- annihilation in His Incarnation; let him look at the Crib; let him go in spirit up to Calvary; let him meditate on the state of death in which He has remained for more than sixteen centuries in the Divine Eucharist, wherever there is an altar in the whole world on which is celebrated the Most Holy Sacrifice of the Mass. Then let him lovingly consider that article of the faith—" For us men, and for our salvation, He came down from Heaven"; and let him see if there be the least semblance, the least shadow, of a reason for doubting His truly desiring the salvation of our souls. Nay, still more; in order utterly to break down and sweep away all difficulties that might present themselves on this subject, He has been pleased, in His love, to oblige us, under pain of incurring His displeasure, to receive His Precious Body in this Its state of mystical death, along with His Soul and His Divinity; as though He would say to us, O poor soul, why are You troubled? Can You fear that I will not give You My Paradise, when I give You Myself? And, that You may be still more assured, not only do I permit You to receive Me, but I command You to do so, and with a love so urgent that You can not refuse, if it be in Your power to receive Me, without forfeiting My favour and My friendship. Thoughts of reprobation, then, do not come from this God of infinite mercy, but from the enemy of our salvation, out of the envy and rage which he has conceived against our happiness.

It is, however, an undoubted truth that the All Good God permits this trial for the greater advantage of our souls; and we ought to comport ourselves therein pretty much as in temptations against faith. Reasoning in these cases is not good; I mean ordinarily, for persons violently tempted on the subject of predestination. That is a labyrinth to the human mind, from which it will never be able to extricate itself. The secret is to abstract ourselves, as much as we can, from the thoughts which arise on this subject, making no reflections thereon, at least voluntarily, abandoning ourselves without reserve to Divine Providence, without scrutinizing Its designs or decrees, which are infinitely above the reach of our feeble understandings, contented to walk on in the ways of God, and acquit ourselves of our customary duties. The man who was told by a devil, disguised as an angel of light, that he was one of the reprobate, performed an heroic act of pure love, when he took occasion then to serve God with greater diligence and fidelity. " Alas!" He cried, " if by my sins I deserve to be damned, and cannot love God eternally, at least I will love Him ardently in this life. O my soul, since we have but a few short years wherein to love the Divine Goodness, let us love, then, let us love: there is not a moment to lose. Let us make up by the fervor of divine love in this world, for what we shall not be able to do in the other." The devil was thereupon greatly confounded; and this is an excellent mode of doing battle with him—to make use of his temptations in such a way as to advance in virtue.

At any rate, let whatever happen, we ought never to be discouraged, never to be cast down. This rule is a general rule, and admits of no exception. No pretexts, therefore, to which you may have recourse can ever afford real ground for discouragement. Though you should have committed all the sins of all men put together, never be discouraged: remember that forgiveness of sins is one of the articles of the faith. Ponder well this truth, that forgiveness of sins must be believed under pain of eternal damnation. But, you will tell me, I am the greatest sinner in the world; I have been guilty of abuses and profanations of grace, which exceed all possible belief; my life has been one of continual relapses, after having received extraordinary lights and favours from Heaven. No, all this will not exhaust the infinite goodness of a God. True, if we had to do with a finite goodness, like that of creatures, we should have every reason to fear, but it is an Infinite Goodness which is the ground of our hopes: to despair thereof is to do It a signal injury; it is one of the sins against the Holy Ghost. Though you should have only a single moment of life remaining, lose not courage; there is still time to experience the exceeding mercies of the Adorable Jesus.

You will tell me further, that ever since you have been in the service of God you have done nothing but fall: and I, on my part, tell you that, with the assistance of Heaven, you must courageously rise again. If you fall a hundred times, or a thousand times a day, rise again as many times. Take the case of a person on a journey, who is constantly falling: does he not, in fact, with all his falling and getting up again, arrive at last at his journey's end, although he may occupy more time about it than one who proceeds on his way without stumbling, and although he may have much more to go through? But suppose this person, under the pretext of having met with such frequent falls, should remain prostrate in the mire, certainly he would never accomplish his journey, and would inflict on himself the very greatest injury. Apply this to the ways of salvation. Go and avail yourself of your falls, to make all the more progress; and, above all things, let there never be discouragement. But I must warn you not to put off rising from your faults to some time which you had fixed for going to confession. What pleasure can it be to remain in the mud and mire, though it be but for a quarter of an hour? Act so that it may be said of you, " No sooner down than up again." If you reply that you fall even into some considerable faults, assuredly here is great matter for self-humiliation and contrition; but, after all, you have only to seek renewed vigor in the Blood of Jesus Christ, and in the protection of the Mother of Mercy: for myself, I will not cease repeating to you, Never be discouraged.

Thus what many souls that are tempted commonly adduce, when there is put before them the example of saints who have gone through trials similar to those they are themselves enduring—viz., that their sufferings have quite another cause, which is their sins—is no reason at all; for, besides that Saints have often alleged the same reasons during their own trials, the idea that these sufferings are the chastisements of sin ought not to make any one lose courage: on the contrary, there is nothing more capable of animating it. God does not punish the same sin twice over. " Oh, what a joy," said St. Bernard, " that God should execute His wrath upon us in this life, and that we should go down while alive into Hell! " They who go down into Hell in this life will not go down thither in the next.

" By temptation," said that eminent prelate, De Belley, " we are punished after a holy manner." How unjust, then, should we be, if, when temptations press heavy upon us, we were to think ourselves abandoned by God, seeing that it is then that His charity is most constraining. " So far," says St. Jerome, " is this from being a mark of abandonment by God, that, on the contrary, it is a special token of His care over us. Temptation is a sign of election. They who are not proved are reprobated. The devil does not trouble himself to tempt those who are his; he assails only those who are God's: in this resembling mastiffs, who worry only strangers, and not the members of the household. Oh, what consolation, thus to be assured that we are strangers to this dog of hell and the domestics of God. God, according to the greatness of His anger, leaves the sinner to take his ease, and, according to the multitude of His mercies, chastises him in this world, that he may not be lost in the next. When it was revealed to St. Teresa that there was no one in the world who surpassed F. Baltasar Alvarez in sanctity, he was at that very time tormented with doubts of his salvation. When a town is assaulted and bombarded by the enemy, it is a sign that it does not belong to him; and the stronger it is the more soldiers and cannons does he bring against it: once taken, there would no longer be either assault or attack. Courage, then, O soul that are tempted, the great noise that the foe makes outside is a proof that he is not within.

CHAPTER III.

DRYNESS, DARKNESS, DISTRACTIONS, AND REPUGNANCE TO PIOUS EXERCISES.

" God," said St. Teresa, " sometimes puts the soul in a state of such dryness, that it seems as if it had never had in it a particle of virtue." She herself endured this state for some eighteen years, passing through the deserts of the interior life, without being permitted to gather the least flower, even of those that grow therein for the saints. A Father of the Company of Jesus, who perished of cold is the snows of Canada, was never free from dryness of spirit and great interior pains amid all the hardships in which his Apostolic labours involved him. I myself was acquainted with an excellent Carthusian monk, who declared, when he was dying, that from the time of his entrance into holy religion (and he was forty years in that state), he had experienced nothing but aridity in his devotional exercises.

There are souls that walk, not only in deserts, but amid darkness. God sometimes lets a soul be ignorant of its faults, because it could not endure the sight of them; then afterwards He gives it the knowledge of them, and purifies it. We have a signal example of this in St. Catherine of Genoa, who did not perceive certain defects she had, although she was far advanced in the path of perfection; moreover, during many years, she became from day to day more ignorant of the secret operations of God, in order that her grace might retain its purity.

The most holy persons are not exempt from distractions. St. Teresa declares, in the thirtieth chapter of her Life, that sometimes she could not keep her imagination quiet for the space of a Credo. " What," she asks, "would they say who think me good, if they knew of these mental extravagances of mine?" St. Jerome, in his Dialogue against the Luciferians, relates that very often—observe what this Father says—very often during prayer he was walking in imagination along porticos and galleries, or was occupying his mind with calculations of profits and gains, or, carried away by an immodest idea, suffered what it would be shameful to repeat. St. Gregory, in the 10th book of the Morals, teaches that in prayer sometimes Heaven and Hell are intermingled, the mind being elevated to the contemplation of divine things, and at the same time repelled by sinful images. St. Bernard, in his Treatise on the Interior Mansion, chapter 49, makes use of these words:

" When I wish to retire into my own heart, the vileness of carnal desires and the tumult of vices bewilder my thoughts. But the greater the disorder which reigns in my mind, the more I ought to insist and persevere with ardor in prayer."

There are states in which the soul becomes as it were devoid of feeling. St. Teresa records this of herself, declaring that for some time she was insensible to good and evil, like a brute beast. While such a state lasts, a man may truly say with the Prophet (Ps. 72:23), " O Lord, I am become as a beast before Thee." He is deprived of all feeling in the exercise of virtues, which he practices often without knowing that he is doing so. The saintly Mother de Chantal said that this state was a martyrdom; and she added that at times all her feelings and all her powers were marshaled like a mutinous garrison in her heart—because there arise dreadful repugnance and aversions to every kind of good, and to all that is most holy and divine. The great secret in all these ways is clearly to understand—first, that it is not feeling or the want of feeling which renders us pleasing or displeasing to God, but the free action of the will, which cooperates with grace or resists evil by its help, or, on the other hand, abandons itself to evil, letting itself lapse into sin in the exercise of its liberty, and through want of cooperating with the grace which is given it in order to avoid sin. Secondly, that dullness and dryness of spirit are more efficacious means of attaining to divine union than are relishes and consolations, because they have ordinarily less of self-love in them and more of the love of God. And here I must notice an abuse which is very common among devout persons, who make devotion consist in what it does not, and do not recognize it where it is. I have dedicated a chapter to this subject in my book, On the Reign of God in Mental Prayer. Here I will only say that this abuse is of the most serious consequence. For how is it possible to practice devotion in a solid manner, if we make it consist in what it does not? How persevere therein, if we do not make it consist in what it really does? How many of these persons will say to you, "I have no devotion," because they are in a state of dullness and dryness, or of darkness and repugnance to what is good! How many think they have reached a very high point because they enjoy sensible sweetness! Yet often they who think they have no devotion have in fact much, if they are faithful to their exercises, in spite of their insensibilities and aversions. Oh, how good it is to walk by this way, in which nature finds no gratification, and we act for God simply from the love of God! For otherwise why should we persevere in the practice of good, finding as we do no satisfaction therein, and even experiencing much discomfort?

That great servant of God, Father Jogues, of the Company of Jesus, who suffered a cruel death in Canada for the sake of Jesus Christ, seeing himself half-roasted and mangled by the teeth of savages, and observing the fresh tortures which were being prepared for him, underwent a terrible ordeal; for, while enduring unheard of torments exteriorly, he found himself interiorly abandoned, deprived of all consolation and without the least sentiment of piety, to such a degree that it seemed to him that it would be happier for him to be a brute beast, like one he saw before him stripped of its skin, than a human being. Had this great man in your opinion no devotion while in this state? There can be no doubt that he possessed it in an heroic degree: herein resembling his Divine Master, who, amidst the agonies of the Cross, found Himself forsaken by His Father; and then it was that He said (John 29:30) that all was consummated. Our Lord commanded a person of admirable sanctity to recite habitually the rosary of the Blessed Virgin; and yet she invariably felt a great repugnance while saying it, her heart being oppressed with dryness and her mind filled with distractions, while the devil suggested a host of evil imaginations; so that she had great difficulty even in pronouncing the words. But in proportion to the repugnance and difficulty which she experienced, was the fidelity with which she persevered in constantly saying it. And one day, as she was endeavoring to force herself to give a more conscious attention, the most holy Mother of God sweetly intimated to her that she was not to do so. This person at the beginning of her life was overflowing with consolations; but in the course of it and at its close she was deprived of them, and became as one insensible. Consolations are the sweetmeats which we give to little children to mate them eat their bread; they who are stronger and more advanced in age will eat it dry.

With respect to distractions, we must take care not willingly to give way to them, and avoid the causes -of them; which are our attachment to something or other— for attachment to anything produces the recollection of it, the idea of it often recurring to the imagination—or a multiplicity of unnecessary affairs, visits, conversations, which so crowd the mind with images of created things that it is with difficulty we can think of divine. We must, besides, preserve our tranquility, and, while we regret the causes of distraction which we have ourselves heretofore furnished, we must bear their effect as a just punishment from the Divine Justice. In fine, we ought to understand, as St. Teresa says, that the imagination is a volatile faculty, a gadabout whom it is impossible to restrain as one would wish. To make great efforts to fetter it, is to injure our heads and ruin our health: a result of which we ought to beware, seeing that many persona have thereby rendered themselves incapable of applying themselves to any kind of employment for the remainder of their life. The same saint asserts that, after having given the subject careful attention, she found no better remedy for distractions than to despise them, and that we ought to treat the imagination as we would a mad thing: leave it alone, and not trouble ourselves about it. In truth, the care which many take to prevent the imagination from roaming, serves only to make it the more flighty, and, instead of driving away the distractions, to create new ones. Provided the heart is not distracted, do not disquiet yourself: God clearly sees that in the depth of your soul you are engaged in prayer for the love of Him; all these involuntary distractions do not interrupt this intention, although they should continue during the whole time of your prayer: on the contrary, the suffering which they cause, if well endured, unites you more to His Divine goodness than many sweet and sensible affections.

Recollect what I have related of the holy Fathers, who have left on record for all posterity the distractions they suffered, not only from indifferent thoughts, but from impure and other very wicked ideas. This it is that ought to afford thorough consolation to souls that are thus tried; seeing that the greatest saints and Fathers of the Church have been similarly afflicted, and have even left an account thereof in writing, a, proof, by the way, that it is profitable to treat of these distressing ways, as has been already remarked; for God is glorified thereby, and poor afflicted souls are furnished with support and consolation. Alas! Have we reason to wonder that the fire should seize on dry wood, when it acts with such force on that which is green? What aridity, darkness, distractions, and interior pains did not the holy Fathers of the Desert suffer! I may add that the solemnities of the greatest feasts are often the very occasions on which we experience the most dullness and dryness of spirit, in order that we may die the more surely to the love of ourselves and our own satisfaction.

CHAPTER IV.

TEMPTATIONS AGAINST PURITY.

Temptations against purity come from the weakness of nature, in which the fire of concupiscence is kindled by too delicate treatment of the body; by sloth; by non-mortification of the senses, and particularly of the eyes; by soft and luxurious clothing; by too intimate conversation and familiarity between persons of different sex; above all, by friendships in which, though not intrinsically bad, the senses have too large a share, and too much regard is paid to natural qualities, whether of body or mind. Or these temptations come from the very apprehension they inspire; the effect of which is to impress the idea of them more strongly on the imagination; or, again, they proceed from the devil, who suggests them for the purpose either of inducing to sin, or disturbing the soul, or making it give up mental prayer and other practices of virtue.

But the All Good God, who permits these temptations, turns them to His own glory and the good of souls. He acts like gardeners who make carnations, sweet marjoram, and other odoriferous flowers grow on a dung heap. " The rebellions of the sensual appetite," says the great St. Francis de Sales, in the 9th book of The Love of God, "whether it be anger or concupiscence, are left in us for our probation, that we may practice spiritual courage by resisting them." " The more the gold is tried in the furnace," said our Lord to a holy soul, " the purer it is: in like manner, the more chastity is tried in the fiery furnace of concupiscence, to which the soul gives no consent, the purer and fairer it becomes." These temptations are an alarm, which rouses all the virtues: to wit, humility, patience, submission to the Divine will, love of God, faith, hope, and all the other virtues. Was it not this that made the Apostle say (2 Cor. 12:10), that he was strong in his weakness? This is why, when a person of great sanctity entreated the most holy Virgin to deliver a soul which was afflicted with temptations against purity, the Mother of God replied, " No, I will not; I will not do it; it will be one of the fairest flowers in her crown: there is no victory without conflict; if the temptations were removed, with them would go the occasions of fighting, winning many victories, and gaining as many rewards."

This consideration ought to be a great comfort to souls afflicted with these temptations, which, although they incite to sin, never become actual sin, whatever may be their effects, so long as consent is wanting. Mud cast upon sunbeams does not sully them; in like manner impure thoughts cannot stain the soul, if it gives no adhesion thereto. " It would be an error," said St. Francis de Sales, " to imagine that our senses or our sensitive appetites are sin, and an error, condemned by the Church in the case of certain ancient anchorites, who had propounded the opinion that it was possible not only to mortify the passions but entirely to extinguish them. "We can never, then, be guilty, however much the temptation may disturb the inferior region of the soul, and stir into revolt all the passions and all the senses, interior and exterior, if we do not voluntarily yield to the storm.

But what ought to be a subject of great and peculiar consolation to these poor tempted souls is, that these kinds of trials do not prevent the most eminent progress in spiritual ways, but contribute greatly to advancement therein. The venerable Caesar de Bus, founder of the Fathers of Christian Doctrine, was raised to a high degree of sanctity by means of these trials, by which he was grievously tormented during a large portion of his invaluable life, and of which he was the more painfully sensible because, as he was deprived by his blindness of bodily sight, they consequently impressed themselves the more vividly and forcibly on his imagination. The holy foundress of the nuns of the Congregation of Our Lady, Mother Alix Leclerc, called in religion Teresa of Jesus, endured trials of this nature so great as to move us to compassion; St. Peter Celestine was thus afflicted to such a degree that he consulted the Sovereign Pontiff as to whether he should not cease from saying Mass on account of the effects which these temptations produced: but this the Holy Father forbade, enjoining him to continue his customary practice of celebrating the Tremendous Sacrifice of the Altar. St. Jerome was similarly harassed in his old age, and in the manner which he has himself recorded in his writings. Satan even dared to buffet a body so chaste and virginal as that of St. Paul—nay, so pure that it was rapt even to the third Heaven. This is a manifest proof that, to live a divine life, it is not necessary to experience no rebellion of the senses and of nature, since that wonderful Apostle, of whom we learn from Scripture (Gal. 2:20) that he no longer lived, but that it was Jesus who lived in him, was sharply afflicted with a sting of the flesh. Chastity does not consist in a great insensibility, but in resistance to everything which is contrary to perfect purity: by reason of which, says an eminent prelate, it is compared to a lily growing among thorns.

If it be asked what ought to be done on such occasions, all spiritual books are full of holy counsels and salutary remedies for gaining the victory in these combats. Here I will only say that we must fly discreetly the occasions of temptation. If saints in their old age and in deserts have undergone these trials, and if some succumbed thereto, this is a clear sign that we have good reason to fear and extremely to distrust ourselves, not relying in any degree on past victories, but being fully persuaded that chastity is a gift of God which is bestowed only on the humble. The proud commonly fall into the sin of impurity. We must be watchful to resist the first beginning of bad thoughts. Suppose a burning coal were to fall on your dress: ah! Would you delay shaking it off? These thoughts are coals from the fire of hell. St. Ignatius, founder of the Company of Jesus, was accustomed to say that the devil was like a serpent, which insinuates its whole body where once it has passed its head; and St. Pachomius related how the devils were constrained and compelled to avow to him that they stood in much fear of those who resisted their temptations at the first outset, and by whom they were at once vigorously repelled, but that they made sport of others who were negligent.

However, we must say, with St. Teresa (in the Second Chamber of the Interior Castle), that our Lord often permits bad thoughts to afflict us without our being able to drive them away: at such times we must be neither saddened nor disquieted. It is enough that our will have no part therein. "We ought to have recourse to prayer, and cherish devotion to the Virgin of virgins, especially to the mystery of her Immaculate Conception, whence miraculous aids are seen evidently to flow. It is good to bless and praise St. Joachim and St. Anne, saying to them that the most holy Virgin, their blessed daughter, proceeded from them without stain of original sin. A person of admirable virtue received extraordinary assistance in the case of horrible temptations against purity, caused by magicians and sorcerers, by honouring the holy Virgin and her glorious parents in this manner. Devotion to the holy Angels, the friends of the chaste, is also exceedingly efficacious. Having done all this, we must remain at peace, after the example of the great

Apostle. St. Francis de Sales, in his treatise on The Love of God (book 9. chapter 7.), expresses himself as follows:—" That sting of the flesh, the angel of Satan, sharply pricked St. Paul, in order to precipitate him into sin. The afflicted Apostle endured it as a shameful and infamous outrage: this is why he called it a buffet, a blow on the face, and besought God that He would be pleased to deliver him from it. But God answered, ' O Paul, My grace is sufficient for You, and My power is made perfect in infirmity.' In which this great saint acquiescing, said, ' Gladly will I therefore glory in my infirmities, that the power of Jesus Christ may dwell in me'" (2 Cor. 12:7-9). Observe: not only ought we not to disquiet ourselves in our temptations, but we ought to glory in being weak, in order that the power of God may be made manifest, upholding us in our feebleness.

CHAPTER V.

OF DOUBTS AND SCRUPLES.

No temptations, of however bad a kind they may be, can render us guilty, so long as they continue to be displeasing to us, any more than our understanding is sullied by the knowledge it may have of the greatest crimes that are committed in the world. " Do you see that looking glass?" says the illustrious Bishop De Belley, in his Spiritual Conflict. " It simply represents the thing that is before it, but the thing itself is not in the glass: it is the same with our heart. It is a glass, in which the devil by his artifices can represent all that is most hideous, most filthy, and most abominable in hell; but it is the will alone that can open the gate and give these accursed things entrance. Let the devil make as many grimaces as he pleases, let him present before your heart the very foulest images, let him whisper into the ears of your interior the most detestable impieties and blasphemies imaginable,—all these things cannot make you guilty. ' Even though these temptations should last all our life,' said our Blessed Father, St. Francis de Sale?, ' They could not soil us with the slightest sin.' You will say that you dread only your own feelings; and I, on my part, maintain, in accord with all theology, which is far more surely grounded than your apprehensions, that it is as possible to unite doubt -with consent as the certain with the uncertain; because consent presupposes an acquiescence of the soul so entire, and a determination so absolute, that it leaves behind it no doubt. The surest mark of not having consented, is the doubt whether we have consented. I would not attribute mortal sin to any determination of the will, except such as left no doubt of its malice. ' Yes,' you will reply, ' as many temptations and crosses as you please, provided I do not offend God.' But is it possible that you do not see that what you are flying from is this painful impression? And here it is that self-love plays its part, and craftily deceives you. Humble yourself before God, and acknowledge that He knows better what is needful for you than you do yourself." Thus far the words of that great bishop.

Scrupulous persons are very subject to these doubts; and their scruples, according to Luis de Granada, arise either from an inability to discriminate between the thought and the consent of the will—for which the only remedy is obedience and deference to the judgment of one's director—or from not sufficiently realizing the goodness of God and the exceeding desire which He has to save us. They treat Him as a stern, tyrannical judge, and thus do infinite injustice to the Divine goodness, being very far indeed from entertaining such sentiments as they ought to have regarding it. These are the very words of that author. This being so, we ought, as the Holy Spirit bids us

(Wisdom 1:1), to think lovingly of the God of all goodness, and seek Him in simplicity of heart. In truth, scrupulous persons entertain thoughts concerning the dealings of God which they could not have in regard to any good sort of man without doing him a wrong. They feel as though God were watching only how to affect their ruin. Oh, how infinitely do His mercies surpass all we can possibly conceive!

Scruples sometimes proceed from a melancholy temperament; in which state a person has need of innocent recreations or medical aid; or they proceed from the nature of the mind, in which case it is not easy to find a remedy; nevertheless, the submission of the judgment will effect much. Scruples also come from the perusal of theological works, especially such as treat of predestination, grace, or other subjects which are neither suitable nor necessary for those who occupy themselves therewith, whether in the way of reading or of conversation; as is the case with women or with men whose state in life does not oblige them to study these matters. Under these circumstances, there is no other way except absolutely to renounce this kind of reading, to part with the books which treat of such subjects, to take no share in conversations into which they are introduced, never to dwell voluntarily on any reasoning or reflections which are suggested by them, putting them quietly out of our thoughts, or, at least, not thinking of them with direct consciousness, or giving them occasion to arise in our minds: otherwise this sort of curiosity is followed by strange torments and sufferings, and experience proves that minds of this sort, which are naturally inquisitive, are always uncomfortable and never in perfect repose. Scruples also proceed from a particular appointment of God, in order to purify and humble the mind. In this state, the remedy is patience and submission to the dispensations of God.

They come also from the devil, who suggests them for the purpose of causing discouragement and despondency, and rendering devotion intolerable; and he must be resisted. They may also be occasioned, or increased, by timid directors, of little resolution and experience: when this happens, it is indispensably necessary to change one's confessor; in a case of this kind there is no room for hesitation.

And here it is impossible to say how needful it is that a director should be experienced in these ways: they -who have only science may do harm in many cases; for, besides the general knowledge which science imparts with respect to the difference between thought and the consent of the will, it is necessary to perceive clearly what passes in the interior of the person who seeks advice, not only by means of what may be learned from himself—who commonly thinks that he does things in a way quite different from that in which he really does them—but also by a long experience of these states, which enables us to judge of them in a manner altogether different from that which would be possible without such experience. It is necessary to have lights such as may qualify us to come to the aid of these afflicted souls—in order to understand what they cannot explain; to say to them what they do not say themselves; to discern their interior operations, as to which they are quite blind; to see clearly in the midst of all this darkness; to inspire them with confidence where they have nothing but fears, and fortify them where they do nothing but doubt and tremble. In fine, there is need of a director full of an extraordinary charity, enabling him gently to bear with the scruples of these persons, which are sometimes ridiculous, unreasonable, and groundless, or unseemly, on account of the extravagant ideas which they suggest, or repulsive from their obstinacy, which is the usual fault.

All this calls for a charity of a very high degree. " There are souls," says St. Teresa, " which are afflicted enough already, and do not need to be more afflicted; otherwise their heart becomes closed up, they are thrown into a state of extreme dejection and discouragement; and sometimes these rebuffs and severities tempt them to despair." St. Ignatius, who was severely tried with scruples, was tempted one day to throw himself down from the top of a house, so terrible was the pain that oppressed him. How many times was he tempted to quit the ways of perfection, the devil suggesting that he should return to an ordinary life, which he represented to him as not subject to all these trials! There have been instances of the finest intellects, great theologians, men capable of solving the most difficult problems, falling into scruples. I have known some who were endowed with a solid judgment, who were wanting neither in lights nor in learning, and yet were harassed in a manner which would have seemed almost incredible, their scruples being about the merest trifles and nonentities. But as to one who is not tempted, what does he know? Let those who feel the most confident be assured that if God were to abandon them to these temptations, in however slight a degree, they would often become more ridiculous than those whom they have a difficulty in enduring. Nevertheless, charity ought to be accompanied with a certain firmness, in order not to furnish fresh occasions for their scruples; never permitting them, for example, to reiterate their confessions, and such like things, of which I am going to speak.

In the first place, general confessions are in nowise suitable for them when they have already made one. They think that the repetition will rid them of their troubles, but in this they greatly deceive themselves. St. Francis Xavier, speaking of these confessions, said that they planted ten scruples in the place of one there was before. Neither does any blessing attend them; the real motive which urges persons to make them being nothing but the love of self and of their own comfort, although fair pretexts of conscience are not wanting. Therefore for persons in this state to reiterate general confessions is to displease God; and directors ought to prevent it. Such confessions, though made only once a year, are not profitable to such persons. They ought to be prohibited from going twice to confession before communicating, for they are tempted to return several times under the idea that they have never acquitted themselves well. They ought to be enjoined not to come a second time, even though they should think that they had forgotten some sin: it is sufficient for them to mention it in their next confession. Their director ought to persist in making them go to Communion when he judges it proper they should do so, obliging them to disregard all the difficulties which their imagination conjures up.

Secondly, it is an excellent rule for such persons to pass over all those sins which they have any doubt about; for, although they who enjoy great freedom of spirit ought to accuse themselves of such sins, yet these persons ought not, because they are under no obligation to do so. When this rule is well observed, the confessions of such persons, which would have extended to a wearisome length, will be soon made; for you will find that they scarcely ever accuse themselves of any sin of which they are quite certain. To say that they accuse themselves for the sake of greater security, is not to allege a good reason; for, since God has laid no obligation upon them and, on the other hand, such a proceeding is not suitable to their state, all this is nothing but self-love. Care must be taken that these persons do not persist in mentioning their temptations, when they see that they are prevented from accusing themselves of what is doubtful, seeing that they easily fancy that they have given a full consent to sin. This is why masters of the spiritual life say that they ought not to be credited, or permitted to confess their temptations, unless they are so certain of having consented thereto with perfect freedom of the will, that they could swear it on the Holy Gospels. They ought to avoid long examinations of conscience, in which they always exceed due bounds; their state requires very little, and they have only too many views concerning their faults. Let them remember that confession was not instituted to be a burden to consciences, as say the heretics, but to be a relief; that all which God requires of us is to confess in good faith whatever we recollect after a reasonable examination, without willingly concealing anything; that God pardons the sins we have forgotten equally with those of which we accuse ourselves: otherwise, persons whose memory is defective would be bound to do the impossible. For the rest, we ought to abide tranquilly by the advice of a prudent confessor; for even supposing he should be deceived, in obeying him we act with a safe conscience. Thus, for example, in case any one should doubt of the validity of his general confession, or of any other confessions, if a prudent confessor judges that they have been well made, he ought to acquiesce in the opinion given; and though the confessor should be absolutely mistaken, and there had been real defects in his confessions, he who thus obeys would not have to answer for them before God, nor would he be the less pleasing in His eyes.

In the third place, then, we ought, above all things, to avoid attachment to our own judgment, renounce our own ideas, and not allow ourselves to be guided by our own views. We must not choose remedies for ourselves; for this is never left to the discretion of the sick. Physicians themselves, when they are indisposed, consult other medical men, and the ablest lawyers seek advice in their own case. Submission of spirit is an absolute necessity, and more is gained by one simple act of obedience than by a thousand inquiries we might institute, and by all the austerities and other devotions we could practice. St. Ignatius, as I have said, being reduced by scruples to a state of indescribable anguish, fasted for eight days together, without taking anything, in order to move the Divine mercy and obtain deliverance from them, but all without avail; whereas one simple act of submission to his confessor freed him from his sufferings. God requires the subjection of the understanding; do what we will, without this our labour is in vain. As for those notions of our not being able to explain ourselves, or that our confessor does not understand us, or has no knowledge of our particular state, they ought to be, despised as subtle inventions of self-love. We must mention with sincerity what passes in our interior, and in such manner as we are able: we are under no obligation to do more. It is the confessor's business to see whether he understands things, and ours to obey him with fidelity.

In fine, we must combat our scruples with generous courage. If they would have us say office over again, or repeat the prayers imposed upon us by way of penance, or hear Mass afresh on days of obligation after having assisted thereat, under the idea that we have not fully complied with the precept of the Church, we must do nothing of the kind. If they suggest to us that we have committed sacrileges in the use of the sacraments of penance and communion, or have been guilty of mortal sin in the performance of certain things, we ought to disregard them, doing everything with courage, whatever repugnance, difficulties, or fears we may experience. If it be objected that an action, however good, is sinful, if done with an erroneous conscience, under the belief that it is wrong, I reply that it is true that when conscience dictates that there is sin in a certain action we have no ground for believing otherwise; but this is not so in the case supposed, seeing that a prudent director has declared that there is no sin where the person afflicted with scruples believes there is. Hence not only does such a person commit no sin in going against his own judgment, but he even performs an act of great perfection. A priest was strongly tempted to despair, because he thought he committed sacrilege every time he celebrated the Most Holy Sacrifice of the Mass; persuading himself, moreover, that he was guilty of sin in almost every action he performed: but in the good Providence of God he was brought into communication with a holy man of great experience, who said to him, " Sir, I exhort you to pay no regard to all these sacrileges which you fancy you commit, and to omit none of these acts which your scruples tell you are great sins, but which, seen in their true light, as prudent persons see them, are not so." He obeyed in all simplicity, despite his own feelings, and by this act of obedience was completely delivered from his troubles. I knew a person who had made several general confessions with the view of rectifying what was invalid in previous ones, but still without finding that peace of conscience which he thought to obtain by repeating his confessions, the first of which, in point of fact, was the only one really necessary. After all this, he insisted on preparing himself afresh for another general confession by a most assiduous examination: and this he spent a long time in doing, writing down full particulars with excessive care. He then made his confession in a private chapel, in order to do so with greater leisure and attention; and having made it he found himself, after all this care and diligence, in greater trouble than ever: nor did he succeed in escaping from it until he had submitted his judgment to that of his confessor, who advised him to make no more of these general confessions, although, as it seemed to him, the very last he had made was also invalid. By this act of submission he obtained wonderful peace of mind; but this was not without having to battle with himself against the temptation to renew his confessions, as, according to his own judgment, he believed that he had never made a good one. God bestowed this peace upon him in reward for his obedience. Without this act of submission, he would have continued in his state of suffering notwithstanding all has trouble and labour of mind.

CHAPTER VI.

OF SUFFERINGS CAUSED BY THE DEVIL.

The temptations which proceed from devils are both ordinary and extraordinary. Their temptations are ordinary when they solicit by means of the world or the sensualities of the flesh. These unhappy spirits make use of the goods of fortune and of nature—as of riches, honours, offices, corporal beauty, fine abilities, and engaging manners—to produce attachment to creatures, and lead into sin; and men, by an ingratitude which is beyond conception, instead of employing the gifts of God to bless Him and praise Him, miserably abuse them: so that the more they are thus favored the more ungrateful they are. For example, if a person is possessed of extraordinary beauty, she will often only love herself the more, and prove all the greater hindrance to others in the ways of salvation. Further, these malicious spirits tempt by means of spiritual goods, either by secretly vitiating the intention of those who have them, or by mixing with them: an alloy of pride and ostentation. Pride, a vice more -common than is supposed, and so much the more dangerous as it is hidden, has undermined the very pillars of the spiritual edifice, and ruined in one moment priceless treasures of the gifts of Heaven.

The devils tempt in an extraordinary way when they .ask God's permission to direct against the soul attacks of a very uncommon character, a permission which God, who is all goodness, does not grant them without bestowing at the same time special graces to resist them. For, indeed, it is an article of faith, most full of consolation, that God is faithful, and will not suffer us to be tempted above our strength: wherefore it is always our own fault if we succumb. A devil said one day to St. Pachomius that, if God permitted them to tempt persons of ordinary virtue as He does those who practice it in an heroic degree, they would not be able to withstand their efforts: but this the infinite mercy of God does not allow them to do.

If the assaults which they direct against the saints be terrible, the supernatural strength with which the saints are endued is marvelous. It is true that it is these eminent souls who are the special objects of their malice, and upon whom they discharge their fury in so appalling a manner. The reason is that they see in them, less of nature and more of grace; they see in them more of God; and this it is that makes them mad with rage. They put themselves to little trouble about others: hence they have little fear of directors and preachers, worthy people though they be, on whom nature has still some hold, through their esteem of talents, worldly goods, honours, distinction, reputation; and against these they raise no great persecutions: but when a man, by a love of contempt, poverty, and suffering, and by complete self-detachment, is filled only -with God, all Hell trembles. Oh, what an object of terror to the infernal crew is one in whom they find God Alone, even though he dwell in a desert, where he can apply himself to no external functions! Here we have the cause of those battles which Hell waged against the ancient solitaries, and which, in truth, were strange and terrible, and almost incessant. Here again we see the reason of that hostility which the devils display against souls that are given to prayer, because prayer is one of the surest and most efficacious means of becoming filled with God Alone.

"All Hell combines," says St. Teresa in the Fifth Chamber of the Interior Castle, "to hinder prayer. It knows the damage to itself that thence results." Observe, this great saint does not say only that legions of devils, or thousands of legions, conspire together to oppose this holy exercise, but all the devils together: a sufficiently clear proof of the very great glory which thence accrues to God and the exceeding benefits which souls derive from this. St. Catherine also says (in the 8th chapter of her Life) that she cannot understand what it is they dread who desire to give themselves to prayer, but that it is the devil who inspires the fears. And elsewhere she says that these fears are sometimes excessive. Let those who are so afraid of the ways of prayer reflect upon these truths, particularly such as cannot tolerate the ways that are highest and most perfect, under the pretext of the abuses which may creep in, and even reject from religious communities those who have greater access to these divine ways; thus furthering, without thinking of what they are doing, the designs of devils. " Strange thing!" Also said our saint: " if a person who practices mental prayer should fall, people cry out in amazement, but they neither cry out nor are amazed at the hundred thousand who perish for want of giving themselves to this holy exercise. The devil tries to divert souls from mental prayer by the example of those with whom the practice of it does not seem to have succeeded; and to this end he endeavors, either to make some eminent person fall into delusion, or to blacken the reputation of those who are possessed of its true spirit. Now here it is that he makes his greatest efforts; disturbing and harassing the soul, in order to fill it with disquietude or disgust, and make it give up prayer altogether, or, at least, to shorten the time it gives to this most holy exercise. Sometimes he causes a very sensible aversion and repugnance to it, by which he afflicts the body and terrifies the mind; and when he perceives that a soul is called to prayer of a simple order, and to the highest degrees of divine union—then it is that he strives the more to keep that soul to what is merely sensible, in order to prevent its quitting these ordinary acts, and make it abide in the conscious exercise of the discursive and other faculties, or to stir up some director who is ignorant of these ways to deter and make it afraid of them; for well does the wretch know what precious stores of grace are to be found in this supernatural state."

Persons, then, who practice prayer of this kind are the special objects of attack on the part of devils, because it is the means by which the soul is most closely united to God Alone, and because it is this plenitude of God Alone which is most dreaded by them. Those who enjoy this plenitude in the highest degree are their greatest enemies, and are assaulted by them in every manner of way, particularly through the persecutions which they excite against them; so that sometimes, as St. Teresa says, they seem to draw all the half-blinded world after them, because everything is done under the pretext of a genuine zeal. But their persecutions are most furious against those who, being filled with God, labour for the reformation of morals and the re-establishment of discipline: the Lives of the Saints abound in such examples. It is well worthy of note, that, finding themselves unable to get the better of Christ's labourers by means of the persecutions which they have evoked against them on the part of men, they will endeavour to intimidate them by strange noises in the places where these persons dwell, by spectral apparitions, by the great terrors they inspire, by the obsessions or possessions of those over whom they have power. This mode of combating by means of obsessions or possessions is the most dangerous of all, and that which commonly serves their purpose best; either because they who are laboring for the reformation of morals become alarmed at the consequences that may ensue, and, not looking sufficiently to God Alone, relinquish their designs—and a very great evil it is thus to yield to the devil—or because they do not avail themselves of grace as they ought. I have had much experience of these dangerous temptations on the part of devils in several places where strenuous endeavors were being made to adopt the holiest means for maintaining the interests of God Alone. Scarcely had that great servant of God, Father de Mattaincourt, taken possession of his cure when a great number of his parishioners became possessed, the demons giving vent to their fury in every manner they could. When the devil cannot do anything else, he afflicts the body. He seized St. Ignatius, and would have strangled him. He tried to choke the seraphic Teresa; and they came rushing upon her in legions to maltreat her. What did not her holy coadjutor in her work of reform suffer from them, that man of God Alone, the Venerable Father John of the Cross! They threw down part of a wall on one of the saint's nephews, who was crushed by it; and they overturned another wall upon a Lay-Sister, causing her death. In the Convent of Alva these wretches fractured a nun's foot, and they lifted another from the ground as she was leaving the refectory, beating her unceasingly all the while: but our Lord appeared armed with scourges of fire to chastise them. In fine, we have seen how they gathered together to conspire against that holy reform of Mount Carmel, employing every means to thwart it. But, for all this, their greatest temptations are certainly directed against the interior. It is not the inferior. I mean the sensitive, part of the soul alone which is harassed and tormented, but also the higher and reasonable part; and, not to speak as from myself on the subject of these kinds of sufferings, which might amaze such as are ignorant of them, or those directors who have not all the experience one would wish them to have, I will relate what the masters of the interior life say of them, and in particular what a learned and spiritual author has written concerning them. The temptation, says this author, sometimes becomes so violent, that the soul feels itself full of all the malice of Hell. Interiorly, it has an aversion to God, to superiors, to good people; 'it is wholly filled with blasphemies, and feels itself so identified with such ideas that it seems as if it were incapable of rejecting them. Exteriorly, it is tormented by phantoms and horrible visions, and sometimes by actual blows and extraordinary maladies. At times the devils form articulate words, making the mouth give utterance to blasphemies, as though it was the soul itself which produced them. Sometimes they deaden all the faculties, or so obfuscate the understanding that the will has no longer the use of its liberty. They mix themselves up with the passions, the humors, the imagination, and excite to vice and fury like those of the reprobate. If the soul desires to perform some spiritual exercise, it is filled with abominations which it is unable to dispel. In certain states they so enthrall the soul that it seems to itself to sin at every moment; and they keep themselves concealed, in order that it may believe that it is itself alone that does it all. They impress it with a strong conviction that in all this it is acting freely, in order to drive it wholly to despair; and it would be almost impossible to persuade it to the contrary. It does not perceive what God is operating within it in its supreme, or highest region. It sees nothing but what is abominable and execrable. In fine, it fares with this soul as St. Teresa says: the devil plays with it as with a pincushion.

Such, concisely stated, are some of the extraordinary pains produced by devils, who tempt men in so many different ways that it is not possible to enumerate them. In my book on Devotion to the Nine Choirs of Holy Angels I have dedicated a chapter to their various temptations, of which I have not room to treat here. I will only say that there is no artifice which they do not employ, especially in the case of those who give themselves generously to the service of God. They strive to render devotion intolerable to them by the disturbances they cause them, suggesting that it is possible to save one's soul more comfortably in a more ordinary way. It was thus they tempted St. Ignatius, as has been said: they represented to him that it is not so necessary to mortify yourself; and this was also a temptation with which they plied St. Francis. They urge people on to do good works and embrace vocations to which God is not calling them; while, under the pretext of higher virtue, they turn them aside from the ways to which they are called. When they see a soul firmly resolved to serve God without reserve, then they labour to push it on, mixing themselves up in the ways of God, and making it proceed with too much eagerness and precipitation, or inducing it to practice excessive mortifications) which ruin the health and render it unfit for the duties of its state. If they perceive an inclination for extraordinary things, they transform themselves into angels of light: they will even assume the appearance of our Lord, of the Blessed Virgin, or of Saints, in order to betray the soul into some illusion; and, the better to succeed in their artifices, they will encourage the performance of a number of good works; they will make known true things that were hidden, and will foretell by their powers of conjecture, which are prodigious, things which seem as if they could only have been predicted by the Spirit of God; and, what is worthy of observation, they will foretell things—and the same happens sometimes

142

even to astrologers— which could not be known except by divine revelation, God permitting this as a just punishment of those who place their reliance on extraordinary things. We have the guidance of faith, which cannot deceive us, and with this we ought to rest content. The human mind cannot conceive the subtlety of these crafty spirits, who will often speak against themselves, and say that ready credence ought not to be given to demonical visions; appearing as angels of light, they will praise and commend such as have treated with scorn the illusions of other devils, in order that they may impose upon souls with the greater facility. Sometimes even those who are following a good direction, and their directors themselves, eminent though they may be, will be thus deceived. There have been holy persons who were frequently deluded by visions and revelations of this kind, against which we can never be too much upon our guard.

And now, what is the remedy against all these temptations? We must beware of lending assistance to devils by the liberties we allow ourselves, the conversations in which we indulge, and our neglect of mortification. "It is our attachments," says St. Teresa, " that give them a hold upon us, and we ourselves supply them with arms wherewith to combat us: to wit, our honours, our pleasures, our riches." Alas! Many holy persons, who have fled from all these things, have none the less been vanquished. What, then, can we expect to do, who are far from having their strength, and are full of nothing but weaknesses and defects? The great St. Anthony strongly recommended fasting, holy vigils, prayer, and, above all, an ardent love for our Lord Jesus Christ, as the means of triumphing over the evil spirits. Our Master said (Matt. 17:20) that there are some which are not cast out except by prayer and fasting. Devotion to the Blessed Virgin and to the holy Angels is also of marvelous efficacy against all their assaults.

As for persons who are tormented with extraordinary temptations, like those which we have mentioned, they have need of a wonderful patience, by reason of the great contests they have to go through. They must endeavour not to follow the bent of their humor, by imprudently shutting themselves up within themselves, and concentrating their minds on their sufferings; they ought to take pains to prevent, if possible, anything appearing externally: I say, if possible; and try not to contemplate their own sufferings, seeing that such attention only plunges the soul deeper into them. This is to be understood of attention "which is voluntary. But they ought, as much as possible, to avoid all introversion and reflection, and abandon themselves to the Divine guidance, by an unreserved acceptance of all sorts of crosses, with no other consideration but this alone: God is worthy of our service, even though we had to endure the pains of Hell. One who was sorely tried by devils said, " If you spare me the slightest blow which God wills that you should deal me, may His wrath fall upon you and augment your torments." To arrive at this, you must attain to a holy hatred of yourself, having no more care for self than if it had no existence. You must desire to see only what God shows you, and to be only what God makes you to be. In these states, fidelity is extremely necessary; the least voluntary remissness gives the devils great power, and the commission of the slightest infidelity causes great difficulties to be experienced in acting aright. Above all, there is need of a profound humility, which fills the devils with rage; humbling ourselves beneath even them, as being the instruments of Divine justice, and being firmly persuaded that we deserve far greater torments than those we are enduring: which, indeed, is most true. One temptation with which persons thus afflicted are commonly beset, is to desire to find rest and to ponder over the means of securing it; but this serves only to increase their sufferings. God requires of the soul a perfect abandonment to all His designs, without exception and without reserve.

For the rest, if an experienced director is necessary in all the different spiritual ways, he is indispensably needed in this state. As it is a state which involves the greatest sufferings which it is possible to endure in this world, so there is the greatest necessity of being largely assisted therein, although it is very rare to meet with persons who are fitted for the office. They ought to be very enlightened; otherwise they will mistake the operations of the devil for those of his victims, which would be enough to drive them to despair. For if these persons were acting by their own movement and with their full liberty, they would be the most impious and abominable of creatures: which is very far from being the case with these poor souls, who belong to God, and love Him, although they are not themselves aware of it. This becomes apparent in those short intervals during which they are in possession of their liberty; for then we see how distressed they are at the offence done to God, and what an anxious desire they have to serve Him. One of the signs they give that they are not free is the violent aversion they sometimes take for those who labour for their salvation, or who are good Christian people, against whom they will on occasions give vent to a thousand insults and imprecations; for it is certain that at the bottom of their hearts they respect them, as indeed they abundantly evince when the devils allow them the smallest respite.

We ought to reason in the same way respecting what passes in their interior against God. I have known persons who were afflicted in this manner for many years, and in whom it was difficult to discover any voluntary sin, because they had not ordinarily the use of their liberty. However, as they think they have, and as the devils themselves do their utmost to make them believe so, they are obstinate in maintaining that they consent with the full determination of their will to all the abominations which come into their minds. This is a reason why their director ought to be a man of great enlightenment; and it is related of Father Coton, of the Company of Jesus, that he met one day with a woman who was possessed, on examining into whose state he became fully convinced that in all the assaults which the devils directed against her she did not sin in any manner of way, although the majority of those who had previously seen her had decided that she yielded her free consent. It is necessary also to watch and seize our opportunity to give such persons sacramental absolution, which the devils dread extremely, and to get them to make a rapid act of contrition, because the devils, the instant they perceive what is passing, deprive them of their liberty. This, indeed, is of frequent occurrence; the persons possessed exclaiming that they do not wish for absolution: all which need cause us little trouble, seeing that these exclamations come from, the operation of the evil spirits.

There is need, moreover, of a cordial charity, a long enduring patience, and a great gentleness, to sustain, fortify, and console these souls. Our Lord, Very God as He was, having been pleased to permit the devil to take Him, and bear Him, and hold Him in his arms, to do with Him as he would, carrying Him aloft and transporting Him to divers places, it is no matter of astonishment if He permits him to exercise power over the faithful, who ought to have a very special devotion to the mystery of the Temptation of this gracious Saviour. There have been saints who became possessed a few days before their death. If this state be one of the most humiliating and the most distressing, it is also one of the most effectual for attaining to a high degree of sanctity. If they who are thus afflicted suffer for their sins, let them none the less console themselves: it is a mark of their salvation. God, who chastises them by means of devils in this life, will mercifully deliver them from their tyranny in the other. O what grace, what mercy, what consolation, to see infinite and eternal torments changed into pains which shall so soon pass away! Let them look to God in their sufferings, being assured that the devils can do nothing without His leave; as is plainly to be seen in Scripture, which teaches us that the devil could not tempt Job without a special permission. This being so, again I say what consolation! Let us be assured that this Father of Mercies never permits us to be afflicted in this wise except for our greater good; but this we do not see; on the contrary, it seems to us quite otherwise: enough, however, that it is so in the eyes of God—this ought to satisfy us fully. "We ought, then, to possess ourselves in great patience, and not contend with our own thoughts, but pay them no attention, and constrain our minds to keep silence, retreating into the centre of our own soul, so that the devil may not know what passes within us. Oh, what fruit we ought to derive from this mode of proceeding, if we make good use of it!

In fine, it is necessary to have a great courage; I do not say to feel it, for so far as feeling is concerned there is nothing but depression and despondency. St. Teresa said that when she reflected that the devils were the slaves of the Lord whom she served, she asked herself, "Why shall I not have strength to encounter all the powers of Hell?" She declared, moreover, that she had no fear of those words: " Devil, devil," when she could say, "God, God"; and that she was more afraid of those persons who had a dread of devils, like certain confessors. Our Lord, indeed, said to her one day, " What do you fear? Am I not Almighty?" These words, cries the saint, are sufficient to make one undertake great works. And in truth, seeing that we have so mighty a King, who is all-powerful, what reason have we to fear? The devil, as St. Anthony testifies, flees before resolute souls; and this is in accordance with Scripture, which says (James 4:7), " Resist the devil, and he will fly from you." The contempt with which we treat him, keeps him in check and weakens his forces.

Anyhow, it is most certain that the devils have no power over the free will, which always remains free, although, as has been said, they may sometimes hinder its free exercise. For this reason it is that magicians or sorcerers can never, by their magical practices, compel the will to sin. True it is that such practices produce an extraordinary inclination thereto, and cause violent temptations: and this is why people for the most part allow themselves to give way, because there are few who are faithful to grace in the mortification of their passions, especially when they press them strongly. And yet there is no temptation; whatever it may be, though all the devils of Hell and all their accomplices should conspire together to accomplish our fall, over which it is not possible to triumph by the aid of our Lord. The evil is that we do not have sufficient recourse to the divine means with which He furnishes us—the sacraments, penance, fasting, prayer, and other exercises of virtue—and are not sufficiently on the watch to overcome our inclinations. How often have magicians used their utmost endeavors to induce persons to consent to sin, and have never been able to succeed! Of this we have an illustrious example in the person of St. Justina the martyr.

Now of all the means that are most efficacious against the assaults of devils, the reception of the sacrament of the Eucharist is the most powerful. Possessed persons, says

Father Surin, of the Company of Jesus, in his Spiritual Catechism, are assisted by relics, but, above all, by the Most Holy Eucharist, which is a rampart of defense against all supernatural evils, and even natural also. The fury which the devils display when the possessed communicate, the torments which they make them undergo on the day they receive Holy Communion, are evident signs of the damage that is done them, and of the great benefits which souls thence derive. Experience also shows that, in order to prevent their availing themselves of this divine remedy, they will leave their victims at peace for some time, when they abstain from receiving Holy Communion, endeavoring thus to deceive them by means of this false tranquility. For this reason directors ought to take care not to deprive these poor souls of this divine nourishment, which is God Himself, and to implore His divine mercy for them; going to places of devotion in their behalf, fasting, praying and even doing penance for the disorders which the devil makes them commit, although they are not guilty of them, humbling themselves before God for the haughtiness of these proud spirits, and studying how to give them no hold on these souls through imperfection and sin.

I will conclude this chapter with a remark which I have had occasion to make in the case of persons possessed or obsessed: it is that it is almost impossible to get them to communicate when they have been allowed to deprive themselves of this Sacrament of Love for any length of time. The devils avail themselves of this deprivation to fortify their position in such a manner that it is very difficult to bring them to do so.

CHAPTER VII

OF SUPERNATURAL SUFFERINGS.

All the sufferings which come from men and devils are not to be compared with those which are received immediately from God. It is easy to endure all the contradictions of men and all the assaults of Hell when we enjoy the sensible support and sweetness of grace in our interior; but when God is pleased Himself to afflict us, there is nothing more terrible. Job, the man of all others who suffered with most patience, cries aloud (19:21) and implores his friends to have pity on him, because the hand of God has touched him; and our gracious Saviour testifies publicly and with loud voice to what He suffers (Matt- 27:46), when He is forsaken of His Eternal Father. For this reason it is that the souls which suffer supernatural pains are deserving of compassion; and so much the more that often, all their crosses being interior, they are not perceptible to the eyes of men, and most persons are incapable even of understanding them. There are others, on the contrary—and I have known such —whose exterior crosses are very great and strike terror into the beholder; and yet they suffer very little, on account of the interior sweetness which is granted to them. When our sufferings proceed from creatures, we can receive relief from the Creator, and oftentimes we are sensibly supported; but when it is Himself who afflicts us, where can we find consolation? This cross is indeed appalling.

In matters of this kind I am glad not to speak as from myself. Here is what the Capuchin Father, Simon de Bourg, says of these sufferings:—" The soul feels herself wholly immersed in the corruption of nature, through the sensible revolt of her passions, the distaste she feels for God, and her weariness in spiritual things. An angel of Satan is given her, who torments her with impure imaginations, thoughts of unbelief and blasphemy, and that so violently that sometimes she seems to give them utterance; in fact, to some persons, this does actually happen. She is oppressed with sadness, darkness, scruples. She believes that she has consented to temptations, and is lost. She will not give credit to her confessors; and, as it is God who keeps her supernaturally in this state of suffering, she cannot come out from it until it pleases Him. She meets with directors who are among her tormentors, owing to their lack of experience: for if a man has not been himself tempted, what does he know? They wish to have no more to say to her; they judge her to be weak-minded, and of a melancholy temperament. She is seized with a desire to give up prayer, in which she no longer finds anything but pain.

"The inferior nature having been thus purified, the spirit must be so likewise by the withdrawal of those acts which it produced during its first purgation. It is not enough for it to be deprived of the power of eliciting these acts if it still knows that it loves and is conscious of its love. God lakes from it this perception and consciousness. He wishes us to become invisible to ourselves, as though we no longer existed. He deprives the soul not only of reflective acts, such as she had in the first purgation, but of the power of making many direct acts, and leaves her nothing but submission to His divine will; a submission which is not active but passive, and which she is so far from feeling experimentally that she would even deny that she possessed it. In the first purgation she sometimes produces conscious acts, and makes sensible resistance to temptations; in this second purgation, she resists without any conscious feeling, her operations are only virtual, without cognizance or satisfaction. If she endeavors to raise herself towards God,

151

she feels a weight of intolerable heaviness pressing on her understanding and her will; it seems to her as if all that has passed within her was mere illusion and deceit. Thus it is that the sensitive part of the soul is purified by means of all these different probations, as also by sickness, loss of goods, and afflictions of other kinds. And it is thus that the intellective part is purified, as also by temptations against faith, dread of reprobation, and despair. In such wise also the will is purified, and by other strange torments." Thus far I have given the words of this writer.

Now let us hearken to that great mistress of the interior ways, the seraphic Teresa. She says, in the 30th chapter of her Life, that sometimes we are disquieted by the merest trifles; the soul goes about in quest of relief, and God permits her to find none; it is as if our eyes were bandaged; faith is for the time as though deadened, and so are all the other virtues; if the soul wishes to apply herself to prayer, and retire into solitude, it is only to aggravate her cross. In vain may she seek a remedy in spiritual reading, the pain she endures is like a taste of the torments of hell; conversation is intolerable, because the mind is for the time in a state of disgust, and she feels as though she were savage enough to eat everybody up. Confessors only torment. It seems as if she had lost the power of thinking of anything good, or desiring to make any act of virtue. It avails her little to perform exterior good works. In the 36th chapter she says that she could think of nothing but what was a source of disquiet to her. In the first chapter of the Sixth Chamber of the Interior Castle she adds that it seems to the soul as though she had never been mindful of God, as though she could never make her confessors understand her, and were deceiving them; and whatever may be said to her, it is of no manner of use. The devil persuades her that she is rejected of God; and such a number of things unite in assaulting her with an interior violence so sensible and so intolerable, that she can compare it to nothing but the torments of hell. She receives no consolation either from reading or from prayer. These are sufferings which are indescribable. She is fretful and irritable, solitude wearies her, conversation displeases her, all creatures combine to torment her, as they torment the damned. Such is the language of this great saint, whose doctrine is heavenly doctrine, as the Church has pronounced it to be; and in other places she declares that neither heaven nor earth could give her consolation; the soul feels as though God were against her, as though He rejected and repelled her, as one who can no longer have any access to Him.

I will here subjoin the reflections of a highly spiritual writer, who, in a book which he has published, speaks in this wise:—" The soul seems to herself to be abandoned by God and delivered over to sin: she does not know whether she consents thereto or not. Directors repulse her; they feel doubts about her state, and contradict her. Sometimes she retains a certain feeling for God; at other times she has none at all. Sometimes God suspends her acts of faith. A soul in this state fancies that she takes a pleasure in her repugnance to God; she feels an aversion for those who speak to her of Him.

In dealing with certain souls, God will sometimes withdraw the pains which they are enduring, because they appropriate them to themselves by a secret approbation, and will put them in a state of stupidity; others He will hold suspended, as it were, on a gibbet between life and death, light and darkness; or He will repel them by hindering them from doing anything for Him, and oftentimes permitting what even appears to be opposed to Him. Finally, God will sometimes leave in souls very dear to Him the effects of sin, although He has freed them from its habits and inclinations. There are souls, says Father Surin, in his Spiritual Catechism, who are so immersed in their sufferings, who have such experimental realization of evil and even sensible impression of vices, yet without giving any consent thereto, that it seems to them as though, both within and without, the waters were overwhelming them.

I have known the case of a person, admirable for innocence, and of exalted sanctity, who felt all the malignity, the emotions, and the effects of sin; to wit, of pride, of ambition, of avarice, of impurity, and of anger. When she underwent the emotions of anger, she was all in a state of fury. When she experienced those of avarice, it seemed to her as though she would have wished to have the goods of the whole world. When she endured the sensations of impurity, her imagination was filled with abominable ideas. Thus she endured the dispositions of sinners, and the malediction due to sin. The horror, the dread, the desolation and sadness which accompany sin, pursued her everywhere. God had commissioned all His creatures to treat her with rigor. As it appeared to her, she was completely stripped of all hope of salvation for the future, or of ever emerging from the state in which she was. She had an utter disgust for everything that passed in her own interior, holding no correspondence either with Heaven or with earth, with the Creator or with creatures; and the holy Mother of God gave her to understand that this was death which was planted in her heart, living and struggling there and taking complete possession of it. Our Lord had, ' Part 4. chap. 6., closed the gate to all consolations, human and divine, and had opened it to desolations of every kind. She felt the pains of despair, which deprived her of faith and of hope; that is to say, she had no consciousness of either; for the darkness is so dense and so horrible that the soul knows not where she is, or whether there be a Church, a religion, a faith, or a God. It is as if her eyes were bandaged, and she suffers without knowing the benefit of suffering. The three theological virtues are as though dead. Nature alone makes itself felt. The mind seems to have gone all astray, and to be without light and without reason. The door is shut to everything that could be said towards making it sensible of the blessedness of this state. God retreats into the pure depth of the soul, and leaves the rest almost forsaken. It is like an earthen vessel which is filled with a precious liquor, and yet neither feels nor tastes it.

Nevertheless our Lord revealed to this soul that this state was the greatest boon He had ever bestowed upon her. It is much to be remarked that He wished her to be so deprived of all consolation that He even prevented her thinking of many divine things which might have afforded her relief. This is the state which that holy book, The Following of Christ, calls the "exile of the heart"; for, after having taught that it is no great thing to be deprived of human consolations when we are in the enjoyment of divine, it adds that it is veritably a great thing to be deprived of all consolation, divine and human, and to endure the exile of the heart. O God, what mysteries are sometimes hidden in two or three words of that divine book which we pass over so lightly! The truth of this is most plain from the words I have just quoted. How many there are, even spiritual persons, who continually read them without understanding them! Oh, how few know what is meant by the exile of the heart! A great servant of God, one of the most enlightened of our age, whose memory is held in benediction—I name him to do him honour—the late M. de Bernieres, of the city of Caen, Treasurer of France, confessed to me that he had read them many times but without reflecting upon them, until the late Father Binet, of the Company of Jesus, gave occasion for his doing so by his admirable exposition of them. Ah! God Only is the true fatherland, the true home of the heart: the exile of the heart, then, consists in being banished therefrom; which the soul realizes when she experiences its effects, although in the depth of her interior she was never more intimately united to Him. They who have made a close study of the lives of the saints must be aware that many of them have passed through these terrible trials; and those who have had a lengthened experience of what takes place in the interior of persons who walk in the ways of the spirit cannot possibly be ignorant of them.

CHAPTER VIII.

THE SAME SUBJECT CONTINUED.

" When My Divine Will conducts," said our Lord to a holy soul, " It allows nothing human to remain." God takes away everything, in order to leave the soul nothing which is its own—neither lights nor spiritual sentiments. He abandons the imagination to distractions, and to the other pains described above; He deprives the understanding of its clear perceptions, the will of all relish and of all sensible love. He empties the memory of everything which is not necessary to it, as well in the natural as in the supernatural order. He deprives the soul of the reflective acts of virtues, not cooperating with it to enable it to produce them, although He powerfully concurs in the acts themselves; and thus, being hindered from eliciting reflective acts and left in ignorance of its direct acts, the soul no longer discerns what passes in its superior region. It has not the slightest perception of its conformity to the Divine Will, or of the peace which abides in its centre, or of the faith, hope, and charity which it possesses in an eminent degree. It sees only its own misery, its want of resignation, the pains which it endures, and of which it has full cognizance: thus does the All- good God deal with souls, in order to preserve their virtues in their purity, and to prevent self-love insinuating itself, which creeps in almost everywhere, through the reflections which the soul makes upon them and a certain most subtle and hidden satisfaction which it takes in them. Further, as it is the way of Divine love to vary the crosses which It lays upon us, God augments them in accordance with His designs and His infinite wisdom, putting His own hand thereto; the effect of which is terrible: thus the Son of God, who had not uttered a word for all the torments which earth and hell had heaped upon Him, cries aloud when He is forsaken by His Father, who thus becomes Himself the immediate cause of His interior Passion.

If it be asked, Why all these crosses? I have specified many causes, and will go on to mention others. It is enough to say that one venial sin deserves all the chastisements of this life. But I ask, Why the pains of Purgatory? Is it not the same God who inflicts suffering in this world and in the other? And they are the same souls that suffer. Moreover, this sword that divides the soul and the spirit, penetrating to the very vitals and reaching even to the marrow of the bones, separates from the creature only to unite to the Uncreated. It is related that our Lord said to a holy person, " When I bowed My head towards the earth in expiring, it was to indicate to the faithful that, as earth had been the scene of My sufferings, so must it be that of their sufferings also. Those who draw near to My dolorous Passion My divine love wholly consumes, transforms into Myself, and deifies." Behold the term of all divine annihilations, which is this— that souls should have no independent action of their own, but act only by the spirit of Jesus Christ. They have no longer their own desires, affections, fears, or hopes. They are not free either to live or to die; they act no longer of themselves, but only by the movement of grace. " You promised me," a holy soul once said to our Lord, " the most delightful things imaginable, and I feel nothing of the kind, I see nothing of the kind, and have no belief in anything of the kind." " This is because you are reduced to nothingness," replied our gracious Saviour. But what annihilations are like those of this Divine Master? The torments and ignominies He endured were an abasement with which nothing can be compared; His soul being separated from His body, He was no longer a man,1 and consequently may be said to have been no longer Jesus. For the space of some hours He is numbered among the things that are not. Creatures, even the most holy, are annihilated only as regards their operations: in Jesus the annihilation reached to His very Human Nature, though still united to the Person of the Word. But, O heavens, O earth, what annihilations does not your Sovereign undergo in the Most Holy Sacrament of the Altar! O creature, who are nothing, and ever wishes to be something, either in nature or in grace, behold Your God, who alone is great and the Only All—behold Him in His annihilation in the Divine Eucharist, where He has remained for more than seventeen hundred years throughout the earth, and where He will still abide even to the end of the world, to satisfy the Majesty of His Father, offended by Your proud self-exaltations. Ah, what a voice cries aloud to our hearts, not from earth nor from heaven, but from the God of heaven and earth! God Alone, God Alone, God Alone: down with the creature! Let it never rise from that nothingness which is its place! O crosses, so lovable, so infinitely lovable, which lead thereto and make us evermore abide therein! But oh, detestable and infinitely worthy of all execration, the pleasures, honors, riches, which turn us aside or miserably withdraw us therefrom!

Most true it is that, to enter into this blessed state of divine nothingness, the soul must suffer much; and, because all the efforts which the creature is able to make with the aid of ordinary grace are incapable of introducing it therein, the All good God mercifully comes to its assistance by means of these extraordinary' sufferings; whether they be so in themselves, or that, being of an ordinary kind, as, for instance, corporal maladies, they are inflicted in an extraordinary way. Oh, how little do men comprehend the goodness of our most merciful God! They reckon His dealings to be full of rigor when they are fraught with a mercy that is unspeakable. Sinful men, sick with the great malady of sin, or stained with the marks which it has left, are unable either to heal themselves, or perfectly to purify themselves, by the aid of ordinary remedies. Now, what is it that, in the excess of His charity, God does—that supreme physician of our souls? He lays His own hand thereto; and, because the evil demands the application of painful remedies, we cry aloud and torment ourselves, when we ought lovingly to kiss that divine hand a million times, and melt into tears of thankfulness, because it thus deigns to operate for our sanctification. It is a most singular grace, which demands a special return of gratitude; for the All- merciful God does not bestow the favour of these extraordinary crosses on every one: it is a boon reserved for His dearest friends. How, then, can we complain if he treats us as His favorites? And yet, since these sufferings are most bitter to nature, St. Teresa declares that, if the soul knew what they were before enduring them, she would have great difficulty in accepting them; so true it is that our cowardice is great and our miseries extreme.

Here I must notice a certain error into which many fall, who think they are in these supernatural states of suffering, but are not so. The following are some of the signs by which we may distinguish a passive state of suffering. The first is, if the soul does not find, and does not desire to find, the least relish in any worldly things, although tempted to turn to them; for this is a sign that it is united to God: otherwise it would let itself follow the movements of nature. The second is, if it is careful not to offend God, and is fearful of sinning; since, if it did not love God, it would not care about sinning. The dryness which it then experiences is an aridity, and not a tepidity. The third sign is, if it is unable to meditate as it was wont to do, but finds itself arrested at a general view, a simple regard, without distinguishing anything in particular. The fourth is, if persons of experience declare that its sufferings are those of the passive state. But, in fine, there is as much difference between these sufferings and others as there is between day and night.

What, then, must be done during these states 1 We must adore the Divine Will in such wise as we are able, abandoning ourselves thereto without reserve, regression, or reflection, to endure all the torments which It may please to send us. We must avoid a certain secret desire to escape from these sufferings, which is incompatible with perfect abandonment; moreover, it serves only to increase them, since they are sent for the purpose of taking away all imperfection, and, consequently, this very desire, which is a great one. When the anger of God visits us with its chastisements, -we must receive them with joy, with open arms, and, in short, everything that may befall us, whether from men or from the devils and furies of hell If you fail to adore any one of the strokes which the Divine Will has appointed, the wrath of God comes down upon you and augments your sufferings. This is what a holy soul said to the demons, as I have already mentioned.

But to descend more into particulars as to what we ought

to do during the continuance of these purifying pains, I
will quote the advice which the Capuchin Father, Simon
de Bourg, gives on this subject. In the first purgation of
the inferior region (of which I have treated above) we
must not indulge ourselves with pleasures of the senses,
under pretext of seeking relief, although it is meet that we
should take some appropriate recreation according to the
will of God. We must not force ourselves to make a painful
introversion; this would injure our head, and render it
unfit for prayer. We must accept our sufferings in a loving
spirit, even though they should come upon us on account
of our faults and sins; judging ourselves to deserve all the
evils we endure, and incomparably greater evils, seeing
that we merit hell. We ought to discern God's hand in the
permission which He gives the devils to afflict us. Hold it
for certain that the way of suffering is the best, the purest
and the surest. Account ourselves blessed in that we have
a share in the sufferings of our Saviour. Keep ourselves
at peace in the summit of our soul. Unite ourselves to the
Divine operation in those pains which it is causing corrupt
nature to endure. Acquiesce in a passive state of prayer,
consisting in a simple eye to God, although we may be
unconscious of it, for this is the death of our acts and of
ourselves; working so much the more because we think we
are doing nothing. Finally, we ought humbly to conform
ourselves to the judgment of an experienced director.

In the second purgation of the mind, let not the soul strive
after the sensible presence of God: this would only serve
to redouble its sufferings, and withdraw it from the state
of contemplation in which God is placing it. Let it refrain
from making acts of its own, contented with cooperating,
in its supreme region, with the work which God is effecting
within it, although it may be, not only unconscious that it

thus cooperates, but ready to deny that it does so. Let it not examine itself, for the purpose of judging what is passing in its interior. The holy Mother de Chantal made a vow, amidst all her anguish of soul, never willingly to reflect on herself in order to ascertain what was going on within her. This vow is one which ought not to be imitated, save by the advice of a sage director, who ought scarcely ever to permit it in these states; nevertheless, the soul must enter on the exercise itself with a generous resolution. The sum of the matter is this: we must live without gratification or consolation, without feeling and without sight, without sense of love, because God so wills it. "He makes us live by dying," said the glorious St. Francis de Sales. The soul is then like a sacked palm-tree, which shoots up the more strongly the more it is weighted and bent down. A great prelate, speaking of his interior sufferings, and comparing them to exterior pains, in order to make them more sensibly intelligible, said to his friend, " I'll tell you what—if someone had cured you of your maladies, you ought to summon him into court, to make him restore them to you; so full of profit and advantage are they."

St. Teresa was well aware of these advantages when she declared, in the book of The Way of Perfection, that the soul gains more by accepting sufferings from God's hand then she would in ten years by those of her own choice. " A state of suffering," said a holy person, "is the shortest road to perfection; for it severs more completely, and, consequently, unites the more closely." St. Peter and St. Andrew, appearing to this same person, assured him that of all these states of suffering that which produced the most excellent effects was the privation of all interior consolation; and our Lord Himself—wishing to teach him that it is sufficient that God should see that inner most depth of the soul of which the senses and even the inferior reasonable faculty are not cognizant, and that sometimes the holiest souls should appear in the eyes of men to be just like other persons, not perceiving how widely different they are interiorly—made use of the similitude of a consecrated host, which, if it were placed along with others which were not so, no one could distinguish. Except he who had consecrated it.

PRAYER TO OUR LADY OF MARTYRS.

O Holy Lady, meet indeed it is that Your august and precious name of Mary, among many admirable significations which it bears, should denote a sea, or an assemblage of all waters; for truly Your sorrow is great as the sea; and, like as the sea, in its vast extent, receives into its bosom all rivers and all streams, as Scripture testifies, even so does Your great heart include within its vast capacity all the crosses of the martyrs. Justly, then, does the Church honour You as her worthy Queen; and it is in union with her sentiments that he who is the last and most unworthy of her children, prostrates himself before the throne of Your glories, there to present to You his homage as Your slave, calling You to his aid as the Lady and the Queen of Martyrs. O my good mistress, make me worthy to mingle my tears with thine, and to bear You company, standing upright and firm at the foot of the Cross with thee. Amen.

PART IV.

THE VALUE OF CROSSES.

CHAPTER I.

OF THE CAUSES OF CROSSES.

As I have already spoken of them in many places in this little work, and especially in the 5th Chapter of the 1st Part, where many of the reasons which I adduced to show the advantages of crosses may at the same time serve to indicate the causes of them, it is sufficient hero to say that they are given either in order to chastise us and satisfy the Divine justice, or to purify us, or to sanctify us; and in all these ways it is Divine love which is at work: the love of God for His beloved creature is very great therein, greater than we can possibly conceive. Oh, what blindness not to see this! What hardness of heart not to be sensibly touched by it! What ingratitude to feel no thankfulness! What infidelity not to make a Christian use of it!

We suffer for our sins; and is it not most just? Did we but realize how great a malady sin is, we should not be astonished. It is for sin that the pains of Hell last forever, without end, forever and forever, for all eternity. It is for sin that the fires and flames of Purgatory are enkindled. It was through sin that death entered into the world and all the woes we there behold. Without sin there would have been no death, no disease, no suffering. It is this monster which is the cause of all our evils. Alas! God in Himself is all goodness, and never would have made His creature miserable. But what a mercy it is to give us chastisements in this world, seeing that, if we make good use of them, they will deliver us from- the torments of the other life!

Here it must be remarked that there are persons of eminent sanctity whom God destines to be the victims of His justice, inflicting on them great and frightful sufferings, and using them to loose and deliver a great number of sinners from their crimes and vices. We have an illustrious example of this in that most devout Carmelite Nun of Beaune, Sister Margaret of the Blessed Sacrament, who underwent extreme sufferings for the sins of many; one while suffering for the proud, at another for the covetous, and again for blasphemers; thus becoming a victim of God's justice in behalf of a great number of sinful souls. But we have, above all, the example of Him who is the Saint of saints, yea, Sanctity Itself, who bore all the sins of the world, being laden therewith to satisfy the justice of His Father. O my soul, here let us pause. Consider what is due to sinners, and consequently to ourselves, if the Justice of God deals so rigorously with the innocent, if the Eternal Father spares not His own Son.

Some suffer in order to being washed and purified from sin, from the stains and bad effects which it leaves in our souls. To accomplish this object, there are, as I have said, two sorts of purgation, one active, the other passive. The malice of corrupt nature is so extreme that it cannot be severed from evil save by dint of suffering. If our bodies need so many painful remedies, some of which are indeed excruciating,—as, for example, those which are necessary for the cure of the stone,—our souls have need of far greater sufferings, in order to be delivered from their spiritual evils, which are incomparably greater than all other evils in the world. This is why the All-good God lays His own hand thereto by means of those supernatural pains which He inflicts, as I have said above. It is for this reason that He deprives the soul of consolations, which, owing to their too close association with the body, throw a sort of cloud over the understanding; and this, together with the self-love which insinuates itself therein, prevents our discovering our imperfections. It is for this reason that the soul is crucified with terrible crosses, which are necessary in order to its being purged of its faults, and particularly of certain most hidden faults, of which it has no perception. " I see, O my God," said St. Catherine of Genoa, " that I have robbed You secretly of what belongs to You, and have taken delight in many spiritual graces"; and the history of her life shows how for the space of ten years she was purified, by means of a hidden love of which she was herself ignorant—a love which every day became more and more concealed—from all that subtle fraud of which she had been guilty against that love; and that in this way she had done penance in secret, without knowing the cause of it.

Some suffer for the sanctification of their souls, in which two things are implied: first, a detachment or separation from everything that is impure, inferior, low, and debasing; secondly, an intimate union with God. Now, in proportion as the holiness of God is communicated to the creature, it produces a greater or less degree of union by the general removal of everything which is incompatible with its purity; and this is not effected without very great sufferings: for how is it possible to be divided and severed from oneself without suffering much? This is why the great designs of God regarding those whom He destines to an exalted sanctity are followed by heavy crosses. O what consolation to you who suffer, if only you knew your own blessedness!

In fine, we suffer because we are Christians and members of Jesus Christ, the Adorable Head of His whole mystical body: the reason being that when the head, the heart, or the other principal parts of a body are in pain, all the other members are in pain also. To be truly, then, a member of Jesus Crucified, it is necessary to be fastened to a cross with Him. This is what the great Apostle means when he teaches (Gal. 5:24) that they who are Christ's are crucified.

CHAPTER II

WHY GOD OFTEN DOES NOT HEARKEN TO US WHEN WE PRAY HIM TO DELIVER US FROM OUR SUFFERINGS.

The All good God often does not hearken to the prayers we make to Him to be delivered from our crosses, for the reasons which have been stated; but above all these reasons, and all those which men and even angels could allege, there is one which carries with it absolute conviction, and is irresistible: it is that God is Reason Itself, and Sovereign Reason; and it is impossible for Him not to act reasonably. When, then, He sends us crosses, they are reasonable, and there is not one that happens to us but by His divine appointment; for Scripture assures us that there is no evil in a city which the Lord had not done, and teaches us that a leaf does not fall from the trees, or the smallest .hair from our heads, but by His wise and holy providence. Wherefore, although we may often truly say that we do not know the reasons of our crosses, we can never say there is no reason for them, seeing there are always very good reasons, which we ought to adore and love, without knowing what they are.

On the other hand, if our crosses are just, they are always profitable to us and glorious. This it is which is so exceedingly consoling. They are just, because, as I have said, God necessarily acts with justice and reason, and He cannot do otherwise; but they are always ordained for our greater good, because this same God—there is no other—is truly our Father, and the best of fathers, compared with whom all other fathers, whatever love they may have for their children, do not deserve the name; and He is a Father All-powerful and All-wise. Now being so, we cannot doubt but that He seeks in all things the good of His children, and gives them always what is most profitable for them, nothing being able to prevent Him. It follows, therefore, that if these good things which our Father who is in Heaven gives us, are attended by many sufferings, it is because it is necessary and advantageous for us to be treated in this way. See you that earthly father, who causes his child to be bled in a dangerous illness: he is sensibly affected at seeing the tears of his poor child, who, not being of an age to understand the need there is of his being bled, cries and makes loud lamentations when his little arm is being bound tight with a bandage. Ah! These cries pierce the heart of the poor father, nevertheless he firmly perseveres in applying this painful remedy. If, moved by the lamentations of his child, he were to comply with his wishes, and allow him to die, would not you say—you who read this—that it would be a cruelty for this father, under the circumstances, to yield to the tears of his child? And yet the child screams and struggles and tosses himself violently about, for he thinks of nothing but the little pain he has to suffer, a pain which will soon be over, and does not see the good that is to follow. This is pretty much what we ourselves do under our crosses, which are somewhat painful remedies, it is true, but last only for a short time; life being but as a moment Compared with Eternity; and we see not that eternal weight of immeasurable glory which they work out for us (2 Cor. 4:17).

Let us adore, O my soul, the Cross of our Divine Saviour, who was not heard of the Eternal Father, though He prayed twice, or even thrice, that, if it were possible, the chalice of His Passion might pass from Him. Ah! He gazed upon Him as He hung upon the Cross; He knew well that He was His Son, and His most innocent Son; He knew well what were His sufferings; He loved Him more than it is possible to say; and nevertheless He did not will to deliver Him, but left Him in a state of abandonment most terrible. It is related of the holy Mother de Chantal, that when she was praying one day on account of her sufferings, our Lord said to her, " The Man of Sorrows was not heard; think not, then, that You will be so." " I see well Your crosses," the same Saviour once said to one of His greatest servants, the Father Baltasar Alvarez; " I love You better than You love yourself; it is in My power to deliver You from Your crosses, if I willed, and yet I do not do it." This was enough for this great man. It is easy, indeed, for a soul less enlightened than his to deduce the consequences; but how just it is that we should deduce like consequences in our own sufferings! O my God, how sweet and consoling are they! What repose, what peace of mind do they not produce in us, if only we are willing to make a good use of them!

CHAPTER III.

OF THE ENEMIES OF THE CROSS. AND OF THE STRATAGEMS OF WHICH SELF-LOVE AND THE PRUDENCE OF THE FLESH MAKE USE TO ESCAPE FROM ITS WAYS.

The great Apostle teaches us (Phil. 3:18) that many are the enemies of the Cross; and he spoke often of them, as he says, because he believes that it was necessary to know them in order to beware of them and avoid them. But what is most worthy of observation is that he could not speak of them without weeping, a thing that can hardly be remarked among all the subjects of which he treats in the rest of his Epistles, sublime and miraculous as they are. And here I will say that there is no reason to be astonished at the tears of this Apostolic man; what ought to surprise us is to see that there are Christians who do not share his feelings, and who remain insensible when they ought to shed torrents of tears. If the cross ought to be the daily exercise of Christians, as our Master declares in the Gospel (Luke 9:23); if it is the only hope of the faithful, as the Church sings;1 if the cross in which it behooves us to glory— note these words, "behooves us to glory," and that the Church does not say that it is fitting or is useful, but that "it behoves"—if the cross ought to be all our philosophy and our theology, all our knowledge and our love, is it not a frightful evil for us to set ourselves against it? And how can we help weeping when we think that it has enemies amongst those who make profession of following it and honouring it? How can we fail to speak often of it, in order to detect them? For there are many hidden and covert enemies who are all the more dangerous the less they are perceived.

Your men of the world, wise with this world's wisdom, proud and self-sufficient, your great intellects that are full of their own importance, dainty people who love their ease, who labor only to find gratification for their own mind and body, who are fond of honor and greedy of praise, whose delight is in the applause of men, who long to be esteemed and loved, who stand in fear of creatures, their contradictions and rebuffs, people who are lovers of themselves—these are all so many enemies of the spirit of the Cross, which to them is a hidden mystery which they do not understand and cannot understand, seeing that it is only the spirit of mortification which disposes the soul to the understanding of this secret.

Other enemies of the Cross there are of the politic order, who, being philosophers rather than disciples of a Crucified God-Man, try to reconcile the teaching of the Gospel with the wisdom of this world and the prudence of the flesh; who desire, so they say, that God should be served, but at the same time desire, without saying so, that nature should be humored also, and self-love have wherewithal to feed and satisfy itself. They desire to please God and to please the world, contrary to what the Scripture says (James 4:4), that " the friendship of this world is the enemy of God." Now, there are many of these persons among those who make profession of devotion. There are many among our preachers, directors, and confessors, who are charged with the guidance of souls in the ways of God's service; and hence proceed two great evils. The first is, that a number of persons make no advance in the spiritual way; a number of communities continue to lead a life of softness and relaxation, in ignorance and without love of Evangelical perfection. The second is, that God is robbed of a high honour, and the Church, dioceses, communities, of immense and inestimable blessings, with which they would be replenished if men only attached themselves to God Alone, if they kept Him only in view, trampling under foot all human respect, all reasons of flesh and blood, all esteem and friendship of creatures, caring for nothing but God, and going to Him in good earnest, by the holy ways of the cross, of which I am treating in this little work. But these covert enemies of the cross are not only far removed from the practice of these maxims; but, moreover, they can scarcely tolerate those who are truly crucified to the world: they secretly oppose the way in which they walk; they turn aside souls from following it; they throw suspicion on them; they take part with the world, which is their declared and open enemy, stirring up terrible persecutions against them by circulating a thousand rumors to their disadvantage, and neglecting no means to destroy their influence.

However, these hidden enemies of the Cross are not wanting in plausible reasons, colored with the pretext of promoting the glory of God. They maintain that we ought have a care for our honour, and labour to achieve a high reputation; that birth, riches, honours impart an influence to whatever we say or do; that the esteem of men is necessary to give us access to minds which we desire to influence; that we ought to win the friendship of people, and particularly to stand well with the great, if we wish to succeed; that it is expedient to make friends in order to gain supporters; that our mode of life ought to be such as may procure us distinction and consideration in the world; that contempt, obloquy, and poverty are great obstacles in the way of doing good; that we ought to avoid making a commotion, and leave people quietly to themselves; that these projects for re-establishing ecclesiastical discipline in dioceses or reforming communities trouble peace: thus, if it happens that any one should at the call of God labour for the promotion of discipline among ecclesiastics, or of strict observance in religious houses, or of true devotion among people living in the world, and the devil and men should unite in thwarting and opposing them, and a disturbance should hence arise, immediately it is said that for the sake of peace he ought to desist from his endeavors; and these men of worldly policy will endeavour with all their might to frustrate, so far as it rests with them, the greatest designs of God. It is true that often they do not know what it is they are doing; but, in as much as their blindness is owing to their want of mortification and their uncrucified life, or to their attachment to their own opinions, they are not excusable before God, to whom they will have one day to

172

render a most terrible account of the opposition they have excited, or which they have themselves offered, to the promotion of His divine interests.

In truth, it is very difficult not to weep with the Apostle, when we think of these enemies of the Cross of Christ, particularly when we consider that these wise ones of this world, as the Apostle himself calls them (1 Cor. 3:18), ought not to be ignorant of the conduct of God. We have need of honour and of the esteem of men, say they: now this is the very thing of which a God-Man deprives Himself. We have need of creatures: He is forsaken by them; His most trusty friend denies Him with an oath; one of His disciples betrays Him; the others take to flight; none dare to say they know Him; all seek concealment. We must deliver fine attractive sermons: His discourses are simplicity itself. The friendship of the people is a necessity: they cry out, Let Him be crucified. We ought to have consideration among men: He passes for a fool at court. A high reputation is of great importance: a robber is preferred before Him; He is made the sport of the populace and the laughingstock of Herod's soldiers; and such is the depth of His abjection that He says of Himself (Ps. 21:7) that He is a worm of the earth rather than a man. He is condemned as a criminal before every tribunal; by priests and doctors, by a king, and by a provincial governor. We have need of this world's goods; and He is so poor that He has not where to lay His head. Yet this is the conduct of a God: and assuredly it must be preferred to the notions of unenlightened Christians, although to the Jews it be a stumbling- block and to the Gentiles foolishness.

Now, if God has made use of these means for the promotion of His divine interests, is it possible for His disciples to imagine that they ought to follow other ways, as though they possessed greater wisdom for their guidance? What can we be thinking of? If we consider all that has passed since the first preaching of the

Gospel, we shall see clearly that the Spirit of God, who is ever the same, has accomplished His greatest designs only by means of crosses. If we read all the Lives of the Saints, we shall see whether He has employed any other means in order to raise them to that eminent perfection to which they attained. Has the Gospel been established by other ways in any of the places where it has been preached, or ecclesiastical discipline in dioceses, or reforms in regular orders? I have brought together a host of most touching examples in my book of The Holy Servitude of the Admirable Mother of God. In fine, the Apostle says to the Thessalonians (1 Epis. 2:1, 2), "Yourselves know, brethren, that our entrance in unto you was not in vain, but that we have suffered many things before, and have been shamefully treated." " Do you not marvel," says St. Gregory the Great, "that the Apostle should speak as if he considered that his entrance would have been in vain, unless it had been accompanied with sufferings and ill treatment?" The Father Baltasar Alvarez was clearly of this opinion when, writing to St. Teresa, he said, "I put far from me the thought that your Reverence can glory in aught save crosses. Your sufferings are no surprise to me, for I know what freedom those enjoy in the midst of them who love God; and I have had greater successes in your Reverence's affairs by these means than by those which are judged to be more favorable."

CHAPTER IV.

WE OUGHT TO HAVE A HIGH ESTEEM FOR THE CROSS, AND TO DEEM OURSELVES UNWORTHY OF

IT.

To take a just estimate of the Cross, it would be necessary for us to know what Paradise is, what an eternity of glory is—in a word, what God Himself is; since by separating us from earth, detaching us from creatures, making us renounce ourselves, it gives us a happy entrance into a glorious eternity and puts us in possession of a God. Strive, then, as we may, we can never value our crosses as much as they deserve. St. Teresa declares, in her book of The Way of Perfection, that contemplatives set as much value on sufferings as others do on gold and precious stones. It is certain that a soul truly enlightened will make more account of a right good cross than of all the riches of earth, and of a veritable insult than of all the honours of the world. She would give whatever is most precious on earth, all its crowns, if she had them, for the most shameful humiliations. Ignominy and confusion are dearer to her than all the applause of men: she would rather be loaded with opprobrium, she would rather have mud cast at her wherever she may go, than see herself caressed and held in honourable esteem. I have said elsewhere that a person of eminent piety, deeply penetrated with these sentiments, declared that he should have a difficulty in not consenting to a feeling of self-love if he were taken to- be put to death upon a gibbet on the Place de Greve. " Strange taste this!" Your wise men of the world, your philosophers, will say; but nevertheless it is true that it was eminently the choice of a God-Man, who lived only that He might die upon a gibbet.

Many saints, filled with the light of these truths, have done great penances and made long journeys to holy places to obtain from the All-good God the grace of suffering. Our Lord has revealed that the greatest crosses were gifts which He granted only at the intercession of His most holy Mother. They are special boons reserved for His favorites, who have a greater or less share of them in proportion as they are more or less loved. Was there ever any one on whom the grace of God was poured forth in greater profusion than on Jesus Christ? And at the same time was there ever any one on whom the Justice of God exercised itself with so much rigor? Never was there glory like to His, never were there crosses equal to His. Next to Jesus, never was any one more beloved of God than the most holy "Virgin, and never did any one suffer more.

This being so, it is most clear that we are unworthy of the honour of suffering. " Our sins," said Father de Condren, of holy memory, " far rather deserved that we should have a share in the honours of the world, its pleasures, and its riches "; and, filled with this idea, he exclaimed that he marveled greatly that he was not himself of the number of those who are glorious in the world's eyes; and, in truth, such is often the portion of the reprobate. " Observe," again, said this holy personage, " the Grand Turk is one of the greatest enemies of Jesus Christ, and he is the potentate who enjoys the greatest riches, pleasures, and honours." " The poor," said the Blessed Angela of Foligno, "the abject, the despised—these are the favorites of Jesus Christ, who have the honour of sitting at His table and of eating with Him, nourished by the same meats; for the Son of God was filled full with reproaches and with poverty.' That holy man, Father John of the Cross, knew this well, when, on the Adorable Saviour giving him leave to choose what he would in recompense for the great trials he had undergone for the promotion of His glory, that admirable man replied, " Lord, I ask only to suffer and be despised for Your sake." " The soul," says St. Teresa, in the Sixth Chamber of the Interior Castle, "knows, with every manner of conviction, that she does not deserve to endure for a God even one little suffering; how much less, then, to endure a greater!" Let, therefore, these crucified souls ponder well these truths; in order especially to guard against valuing themselves in consequence, or being betrayed into a certain natural reliance on their states, and being led to foster a secret complacency therein, and a subtle self-esteem.

O my soul, for the remainder of our days let us have nothing but the utmost respect for these ways of the Cross: ways painful to nature, humiliating before men, but most holy in the order of grace, and all glorious in the eyes of God and of His angels. Let us declare ourselves once for all on the side of our
Sovereign Master. Let us, with Him, account those blessed whom the world curses and says all manner of evil against, who are hated, spurned, and thrust aside, whose life is one of sorrow and tears. Let us, with the Spirit of God (Eccles. 7:3), esteem it better to go to the house of mourning than to that of joy. Let all persons, places, houses, that are signed with the sign of the Cross, be to us objects of veneration. Rightly do we reverence the representations of the Cross, which are only of wood or paper; much more, then, let us reverence the living images, which all afflicted Christians are. Whenever we enter houses which the world counts wretched, where we find only families plunged in misery, where we hear nothing but groans and sighs, and behold nothing but poverty and distress, let us pause in reverence. Let us remember that these are the Louvres, the palaces, of God: and do we not know that hospitals, the abodes of sickness and of sorrow, have the privilege of being called the hotels de Dieu ("houses of God")? a singular privilege which is awarded to them alone. O what happiness! If we encountered a person who was an outcast from the world, who knew not, so to say, where to put his head, who was

abandoned and repulsed by good men as well as by bad, forsaken by his kinsmen and nearest friends, who served as a butt and a jest in all companies, and was reduced to extreme destitution through loss of goods, of honour, and of everything that can content the senses—verily, O my soul, in honour of a state so holy we ought to kiss the ground on which he has trod: for, in truth, the Cross, wherever it appears, deserves a veneration peculiarly its own. If we consider our Divine Exemplar, the Adorable Jesus, we shall see that He goes forward to meet His murderers, and courteously forestalls them: it is because they are come to take Him and lead Him to the Cross. Let us, then, receive with profound respect all crosses which befall us; let us sometimes even go forward right courteously to meet them; let us do them honour in ourselves, in all persons, in all places, where ever they appear. Yea, we ought to alight from our horse to do them honour, when we pass before houses of affliction, keeping our head uncovered and all our interior in a state of recollection.

It must, however, be confessed that even among persons of piety there are very few who are faithful to the honour due to crosses. Alas! They wish to have nothing to do either with the Cross or with those who bear it. What they seek is a devotion which is caressed and applauded, approved, esteemed. Persons desiring direction are eager in choosing guides who have gained themselves a name; there is a rush after fashionable preachers, without much consideration as to the effects that result for the interests of God. A few ladies of the world are sufficient to establish their credit. Such men are pleased at having the direction of persons who attract attention on account of the estimation in which they are held. They are delighted at having grand people at their sermon, and at hearing it said, "There were so many carriages, the streets were quite full." O my God, what sort of piety is this! All breathes of nature. After speaking contemptuously of the world and its ways, it likes to find its account in a troop of devout people, whose love it seeks, and whose esteem it is glad to enjoy. Experience shows that we carry self about with us everywhere.

But crucified souls are not pleasing. True it is, there are still some persons who have a respect for them, who assist and stand by them so long as a few more of their fellow-creatures take their part. The hostility of the wicked does not weigh much against them, so long as they have the approbation of the good. The opposition even of a few devout people does not prevent their being well regarded, provided there are others of the same class who hold them in esteem. But when everybody withdraws from them, both the good and the bad, then these retire with the rest: so true it is that there are few who simply look to God alone. Yes, " God Alone," say they; but it is only with the mouth; in practice they must have the creature with Him. They would be ashamed to remain with God alone, they would feel it to be a humiliation and a disgrace openly to take part with a crucified soul, whom all the world despises. Thus this grace is very rare, and is seldom to be found even amongst those who otherwise are far advanced in the ways of God. This grace implies a perfect renunciation of self, entire disengagement; for often the friends of these crucified souls are themselves crucified, and have a share in their sufferings. It demands a magnanimous courage and a Christian generosity; for there is nothing more generous than the Christian spirit. This is why it is an intolerable error to wish to cover the timidity and cowardice of nature under false pretexts of virtue; seeing that virtue is never cowardly when it is true.

Ecclesiastical history is full of marvelous examples

displaying the invincible generosity of the Christian spirit; and it cannot be denied that it shone forth in an admirable manner in certain friends of St. John of Chrysostom, who suffered for defending his cause. The lector Eutropius lost his life on this account, and is reckoned by the Church as a martyr. A number of ladies, despite the weakness of their sex, chose rather to be despoiled of their goods, endure the pains of banishment, and see themselves loaded with injuries and insults, than abandon the defense of their saintly director.

The great Apostle sets so singular a value on Christian generosity that, in his Epistle to the Romans (chap. 16), he makes honorable mention of those who had shown themselves zealous in his cause and had assisted him; he commends them to the brethren and he desires that they may be especially saluted on his behalf; he mentions them by name, to the end that they may become known, not only to the faithful of his own day, but also to Christians of all times, even to the consummation of the world. He speaks (v. 4) of some who had hazarded their very lives for his sake; and he declares that they deserve, not only his own personal acknowledgments, but those of all the Churches. He says that all the Churches of the Gentiles are grateful to them and give them thanks. In his second Epistle to Timothy (1:16, 17) he prays the Lord to show mercy to the house of Onesiphorus, because he had not been ashamed of his (the Apostle's) chains, and, when he came to Rome, had carefully sought him out; which so deeply touched that noble heart that he several times repeats his prayer to the Lord that He would grant him mercy, asking it for himself, his house, and his whole family. Nay, does he not affirm, in this same Epistle to his dear son Timothy (1:7), that God has not given us the spirit of fear, but of power? This is why he declares (v. 8} that he (Timothy) ought not to blush for his bonds, and be ashamed of his person, amidst the humiliations to which he was subjected.

CHAPTER V.

WE OUGHT TO LOVE CROSSES.

Love follows on esteem; we love things in proportion- to the value we set upon them. I have just spoken of the worth of crosses, and this little work abounds in motives most capable of making us perceive their value and urging us to love them. But let me say, in one word, what may carry absolute conviction to the mind, as to the obligation that lies upon us of having a love for crosses. Jesus, God-Man, loved them: therefore they are lovable. He loved them with an ardor inconceivable: therefore they ought to be the objects of our greatest affection. Let men say what they will, though they should all unite together in persuading us to the contrary, we must adhere to the sentiments of a God. All men may be deceived; a God can neither be deceived nor deceive others. They who follow Him walk in the light and in the truth; every other path leads astray and is full of darkness.

The Adorable Jesus, our God, loved sufferings. They were His treasure, His joy, His glory, His sweetness, the delight of His heart, His love. He espouses the Cross at His first entrance into the world: this is why He is the Man of Sorrows; He never quits it, He lives on it, He dies on it. You would say that He has not words choice enough to express His affection for it. He is not content with saying that He desires it, but He declares (Luke 22:15) that He desires it with desire; that is to say, with a desire which angels and men ought to adore, but of which they will never be able to comprehend the greatness. The love of the Cross urges

Him so strongly that, when multitudes of every age and condition thronged about Him, " so that they trod one upon another" (12:1), suddenly He cries aloud, in the midst of a long discourse (v. 50), " I have a baptism wherewith I am to be baptized,"—meaning His Passion—" and how am I straitened until it be accomplished! " Nay, He was so continually occupied with this love, that at the very time He was displaying the splendors of His glory on Thabor, He discoursed (Luke 9:31) concerning the exceeding torments which He was to be made to endure. Nor is this all: so transported is He with the love of the Cross, that He calls (Matt. 16:23) the Prince of the Apostles Satan when, out of His great natural affection, he would have turned Him away therefrom; and He calls (26:50) Judas His friend, when he supplies Him with the occasion of undergoing the sufferings prepared for Him. He bids St. Peter on that occasion to be gone from Him, because he was a scandal unto Him; and He rises and goes to meet the disciple who betrays Him, that He may give him the kiss of peace. Magdalen, she who loved Him so devotedly, shall have only His feet to kiss; John, His privileged favorite, shall have His bosom to rest upon; but His mouth is reserved for Judas. This reflection is made by the author of The Book of the Cross.

How is it possible for us to realize all these truths, and to know how precious and dear the Cross was to Jesus, without ourselves taking fire and being all inflamed with a desire for pains and sufferings? Let us say with the Holy Spirit (Gal. 5:24) that they who are Christ's are crucified. To be a Christian and to bear the cross is one and the same thing. But let us learn of one of the first Christians, a great lover of the cross, the noble way of loving it. It is the glorious St. Andrew of whom I speak. He cries aloud that he has loved it earnestly: his was no idle, careless, easy, tepid love; that it has long been the object of his desires: he has not desired " the day of man," to use the words of Scripture (Jer. 17:16),that is to say, the pleasures and the honours of this present life; that he has sought for it without ceasing: not merely in the transports of a prayer all light and sweetness, and amid the consolations or the pleasurable emotions of a sensible devotion, but amid aridity and repugnance, by day and by night, at all times, on all occasions, and in all sorts of states, without ever relaxing aught of the ardor which made him sigh after it continually. Thus, when he perceives it from afar, he salutes it, he venerates it; and this he does openly before his judges; he is not ashamed of the Gospel. Instantly, as soon as he beholds it, he cries out, like one enraptured— you would think that he was intoxicated with love—and, without caring to consider what men may say, who regard it as accursed, he calls it good and precious; he offers it his homage, and makes his supplications to it. You would say he was going to his bridal; and, indeed, you would not err, for the cross as the nuptial couch of souls that are the spouses of a God-Man. He goes thereto full of joy, with a confidence that knows no bounds; for most true it is that the cross is the sure road to Heaven. He entreats, he conjures with all possible earnestness, the people who wish to save him from it, not to deprive him of this happiness, not to rob him of this glory; and, as he hangs upon it, lingering on for two whole days, he converts this beloved cross into a sacred pulpit, whence to preach to the multitude the divine mysteries of our holy religion. I invite all the lovers of the Cross to come to this school, there to learn, once for all, how to love sufferings in a truly generous way.

CHAPTER VI.

WE OUGHT TO ACCEPT CROSSES WITH JOY, WITH THANKSGIVING, WITH ASTONISHMENT.

He who has a true love for the Cross suffers, not only with patience, but, as St. Bernard observes, even with joy. To act otherwise is to be wanting in faith; for, seeing that faith teaches us that crosses are God's greatest gifts, if we were intimately persuaded of this truth, how could we fail to rejoice on being favored with them? If a great king did you the honour of making you a costly present, would you not be delighted? Would it be necessary to exhort you to patience? And what would this monarch say—nay, what would all the world say—if it were known that you had received this precious gift merely with patience? Hence the Son of God, speaking of the way in which the heaviest crosses ought to be accepted, says to His disciples (Luke 6:23), " Be glad, and leap for joy." The Apostle, entering into the sentiments of his Divine Master, protests (2 Cor. 7 4), not only that he is " filled with comfort," but that he " exceedingly abounds with joy in all his tribulations "; and, speaking of the first Christians, he says (8:2) that " in much experience of tribulation they had abundance of joy." Nay, the Holy Spirit teaches us, in the Epistle of St. James (1:2), that " divers temptations " (or sufferings) afford matter for all sorts of joy. Thus, according to the teaching of the Holy Spirit, crosses ought to be the subject, not only of a great joy, but of " all joy." Let us, then, figure to ourselves the joy of a man who should come into the possession of great riches; or of one who, loving the pleasures of life, should be given to taste of all their seeming delights; or, again, of some obscure person who should be elevated to a throne and presented with a crown. Let us figure to ourselves the joy of merchants when they make great profits in their traffic; of farmers when they gather in an abundant harvest;

of generals when they win battles; of kings when they conquer cities and provinces; of the sick on recovering their health; of captives on being delivered from their chains; of persons deeply afflicted on the cessation of their troubles; and, in fine, all those subjects of joy, without exception, which can happen to persons in general: all these joys ought to be the joys of a crucified soul. Let us, then, no longer be astonished if the Son of God said that when we suffer we ought to leap, or bound for joy. Yea, it would be no exaggeration to say that we ought to die of joy. How many have died from reasons which are utterly worthless, compared with the true, the great, the extraordinary motives for exultation which crosses bring with them!

However, it is true that Christian joy does not depend on anything sensible: it has its seat in the centre of the soul, where often it is not perceived in the inferior region, not even in its reasonable part. It abides there hidden, in order that it may be maintained in all its purity; for its Sowings over into the sensitive region, which sometimes happen, are greatly exposed to the danger of self-love, through the satisfaction which thence proceeds. It is quite compatible with sadness in the inferior region, as is evident in the person of our Lord Jesus Christ. The Apostle, when he says that he exceedingly abounds with joy in all his tribulations, does not the less avow (1 Cor 1:8) that they afflicted him, " out of measure," so that he was " weary even of life ": which shows plainly that we must understand him to mean the joy which is in the supreme region of the soul; otherwise he would be in contradiction with himself. We do not thereby deny that the inferior and sensitive part of his soul had a share therein at certain times; we say only that it is sufficient that the joy should be in the summit of the soul, which finds her satisfaction in the order of God's dealings with her, although, so far as feeling is concerned, she experiences only an overwhelming sadness. Neither does this joy prevent even moderate complaining in the inferior region, when the senses feel nothing but affliction and lament accordingly; our Lord regarding them as little children who cry when they are chastised. To prevent their weeping would be to stifle them. But the effect of this joy is that, despite all our sensations to the contrary, we are delighted at being in a state of suffering, we signify our esteem for it to everyone; we invariably set a great value on crosses, as well on those which befall ourselves as on those which we remark in others. There are even some who on these occasions break out into self-congratulations for having received so great a gift from Heaven. They testify both by voice and in writing the esteem in which they hold it; and they are right in doing so. If people of the world congratulate themselves so much on account of some good fortune that has happened to them, O my God, what a glorious fortune, according to the spirit of Jesus Christ, is that of sufferings! I know that they are hard to nature; but if a miser, said Father Baltasar Alvarez, who had spent much money in cultivating his vineyard, beheld it visited by a hailstorm, doubtless to his great affliction —if, I say, this miser were to learn that the hailstorm was composed of crown-pieces, his affliction would be speedily changed into the sweetest consolation possible. Now, O my soul, let us learn that crosses are so many gold pieces of Heaven's coinage: they are its precious stones.

All these subjects of joy are at the same time subjects of thanksgiving. This is why we must take heed not to be ungrateful for them. As soon, then, as any affliction happens to us, whether of body or of mind, and from whatever quarter it may come, let us instantly fall on our knees to thank Divine Providence for it; and the greater the affliction the greater also ought to be our gratitude, and our zeal in testifying it, whether by having Masses of thanksgiving offered, or by the performance of some good works, such as fasts, pilgrimages, alms deeds, visiting of the sick and of prisoners, and other like practices. That great servant of God, Father John Chrysostom, of the third order of St. Francis, understood this well, seeing that he bound himself by vow to fast a hundred days in honour of St. Joseph, in the hope that through his intercession he might obtain from the All good God the favor of being despised by all the world. On such occasions Christian friends will meet together to unite in thanking God; for they would neglect nothing by which to evince their gratitude. They who are most enlightened will give advice to others on the subject, in order that the gifts of God may not remain unacknowledged. An English nobleman, having lost all his property and being reduced to poverty, had a Te Deum sung in a religious house; and I myself knew a lady who on losing a lawsuit immediately went to have the Holy Mass offered in thanksgiving. If we thank God on being healed of a disease, or on being delivered from some harassing affair, how much more when we are visited by a heavy cross: for if a poor man testifies his gratitude to you for bestowing half-a-crown upon him, what ought he to do if you give him fifty pounds? Now, crosses are Heaven's richest gifts. Often our ingratitude deprives us of them, or causes God to withdraw those which He had sent us, and to abandon us to our pleasures; as He does the Grand Turk, and so many infidel lords, and other reprobate souls who abound in earthly honours and delights.

In fine, if our gracious Saviour treats us as His favorites by not being sparing of crosses to us, have we not reason to be astonished, seeing that we deserve for our sins to be given over to our own desires and the gratifications of nature? O how great ought to be our astonishment, when we consider that the All merciful God sometimes seems to throw everything into confusion in order to accord to us the great happiness of suffering! You will see fathers deserting their children, children ill-treating their parents, husbands ill-using their wives, wives tormenting husbands, your best friends forsaking you, those who are under the greatest obligations to you taking part against you, judges shutting their eyes and deciding unjustly; superiors prejudiced against you, and persisting in their prejudices; worthy people deceived; persons of eminent virtue led into error; witnesses blindfolded; and the devil, as St. Teresa says, drawing all the world after him by the ill reports to which he gives currency. Undoubtedly these heavy blows from Heaven are its strokes of grace. Let us justly be astonished, then, if we are thus honoured, and never cease from our astonishment. The gift of sufferings is too precious a boon for people such as we are. It is fit only for the favorites of a God. Assuredly on these occasions we must be beholden to the Queen of Heaven, the holy angels, or some other saints of Paradise, who have interested themselves in obtaining such graces for us.

CHAPTER VII.

WE MUST CARRY OUR CROSS WITH ALL ITS DIMENSIONS.

Although I have treated at large of the way in which we ought to bear the Cross, nevertheless, since it is a matter on which it is not possible to speak too much, in order to the making a holy use thereof, I will here also say that in bearing our Cross we must take care to bear it with all its dimensions. Of these, as St. Augustine and St. Anselm hold, the Apostle writes to the Ephesians (3:14—19), and accounts them so fraught with mystery that, to be able to comprehend them with all the Saints—for all the Saints have had that knowledge—and to obtain the understanding of them for the faithful to whom he writes, he bows his knees to the Father of our Lord Jesus Christ, that, according to the riches of His glory, He would strengthen them with His might by the Holy Spirit. And most true it is that without the special aid of that Divine Spirit these mysteries will ever remain 'concealed, particularly from the wise and prudent of thus world, who fly from sufferings, and consider that their credit is implicated in doing so.

Looking, then, solely to the light and power of Jesus Christ, which I implore in all humility, bowing myself down in profoundest self-abasement before the Infinite Majesty of the Eternal Father, and which I ask in the might of the Holy Spirit, through the glorious Name of Jesus and those of His blessed Mother, all good angels, and the saints, acknowledging that in myself I am utterly unworthy thereof, I say that we ought to bear the cross with all the dimensions which St. Paul attributes to it—that is to say, its breadth, and length, and height, and depth; and herein especially consists the knowledge of the charity of Jesus Christ, a knowledge to which all human sciences never can attain, but which is given to those in whom the Adorable Jesus dwells by faith, and who are solidly founded and deeply rooted in His love.

Now, by the first dimension of the Cross, which is its breadth, must be understood all the circumstances, effects, and consequences which accompany or follow the crosses which we bear. It is sad to see persons who imagine that they are quite willing to bear the cross—(if they have but a modicum of virtue they would be ashamed to speak and to think otherwise)— but who would wish not to bear this and that cross because of its circumstances or its effects. They

would not mind, they say, being poor: what pains them
is the disgrace, the contempt, the dependence which are
the results of poverty. They would willingly endure their
maladies: what distresses them is that they are prevented
going to church, or performing the usual exercises of the
community: if the sufferer be a preacher or a missionary,
he is incapacitated for doing the good he might otherwise
do; it is an inconvenience to other persons, and a burden;
he becomes useless. They would be content to go to some
other place, to shift their abode, although nature would
suffer thereby: what troubles them is that they will not have
several advantages which they enjoyed elsewhere, and
which seem to be very profitable. They would quite rejoice
at being crucified; but not by certain sorts of temptations
or interior crosses. They would be well pleased to endure
contradictions; but to suffer them from certain persons
nearly related, or under great obligations to them, or for
a fault which they never committed—this it is that hurts
them. Now, all these persons do not see that such thoughts
are suggested by our self-love; that, while it beguiles us
with the esteem and love of crosses which are not laid upon
us, its aim is to prevent our bearing in a Christian way those
which are allotted to us. The crosses which we have are the
crosses which Jesus Christ wishes us to bear, and not those
which we figure to ourselves.

We must bear our Cross, then, with its first dimension,
which is its breadth; that is to say, with whatever
circumstances may attend it. Does not God know what
it is, and does He not clearly see it? Assuredly it was a
most distressing thing to the Blessed Robert d'Artus of
Arbrisselles, to have his character publicly aspersed by
rumors which charged him with being guilty of infamous
crimes such as were committed by the heretical Illuminati.
He was the founder of an Order, and of an Order of nuns as

well as of men; and therefore it seemed as if his reputation were a necessity to him, and so much the more because that Order encountered much opposition; and, indeed, even now we constantly meet with persons who can scarcely divest themselves of a certain prejudice regarding it, though without any solid reason. The accusations brought against him had reference to purity, a circumstance which must have been a sensible affliction to a founder who had the government of nuns. This befell him shortly before his death, at a time when, generally speaking, a man's reputation must be established, if ever it is to be. He suffered especially from Geoffrey, Abbot of Vendome, a noted personage, who wrote him a letter, in which he exhorts this holy man to be more discreet in his conduct towards women; because (as he said) he showed himself harsh to some, even to the extent of afflicting them with hunger, thirst, etc., while with others he was gentle and familiar, even visiting them by night. Nevertheless, this great servant of God and of the most holy Virgin, seeing clearly that this cross, disgraceful as it might be to him, was still his cross, bore it with great serenity, not even making any reply to the letter of the celebrated Abbot of Vendome. His spiritual daughters did not fail nobly to vindicate his character, declaring that the charges brought against him were false, but the man of God abandoned his defense to Divine Providence. I may add that all who are devout to the Blessed Virgin owe him a great debt of gratitude for having established an Order in the Church, the principal object of which is to honor the Maternity of the holy Mother of God, who is the Mother also of all the faithful. It was on this account that he chose to establish that singular regulation by which the monks were placed in a state of dependence on the nuns; in imitation of that of the Beloved Disciple, the glorious St. John the Evangelist, in respect to the Virgin of virgins: a thing which, in truth, is peculiar to this Order, but which is none the less commendable, and, indeed, is so essential to it that —as was aptly remarked by the late Father de Condren, of holy memory, a man who was endowed with lights truly angelical, and a seraphic love, loving God Alone—to change it would be to destroy it, seeing that it was inspired by God in order to honour in the Church with a special cult the Maternity of the holy Virgin and the filiation by adoption of all the faithful in the person of the amiable St. John the Evangelist, a Saint to whom all the children of Mary ought to have a peculiar devotion. I have a chapter on this subject in my book Of the Servitude of the Mother of God.

Again, we must bear our Cross with its second dimension, which is its length; that is to say, its duration, so long as it shall please the All-good God that we should bear it. St. Francis of Assisi was during all his life a man of crosses; but for two years he underwent extraordinary mental sufferings, which sometimes caused him such a feeling of depression in the inferior part of his soul that for the time he could not endure that any of his religious should so much as speak to him. St. Hugh, Bishop of Grenoble, and many other Saints, suffered similar internal pains to the very hour of their death. St. Brigit declares that it was revealed to her from Heaven that the most holy Virgin had the knowledge of her beloved Son's sufferings from His very infancy. St. Teresa says the same, declaring that she had learned it from our Lord by revelation. Thus this Mother of Love became from that time forth a Mother of Sorrows, which she continued to be for the remainder of her most holy life through the abiding thought of Calvary. And indeed the Adorable Jesus Himself was in a continual state of suffering for the space of more than three-and-thirty years, which was, in fact, the whole course of His precious life; and that, too, by day and by night, always and in all places.

This is why in St. Matthew (20:22) He says He will drink of the chalice, of which in St. Mark (10:38) He says that He does drink. And, indeed, certain of the Fathers think that by those words: " My God, My God, why have You forsaken Me?" (Matt 27:46) He testified that He was not yet satiated with the sufferings He had endured; as if He had meant to say, " Why abandon You My body to languores which are leading it to death? Why do You not miraculously strengthen it that, instead of the three and thirty years which I have spent in suffering, I might continue to suffer for many centuries?" Hence we must not be astonished if the glorious St. Francis Xavier, who said to God in his consolations, "Enough, Lord, enough! " said to Him in his sufferings, " Still more, my God, still more! " Or if we find St. Teresa teaching, in the Fifth Chamber of the Interior Castle, that it would be a rest to the soul if the trials we are undergoing were not to cease until the end of the world, suffering as we do for so good a God; or if persons are to be met with, afflicted with terrible crosses, who feel alarmed at the bare thought of being delivered from them, and are affected with a certain sadness when they reflect that the All-merciful God might haply put an end to their sufferings, and make some change in their condition. I have myself been acquainted with persons who frequently felt what I have here described; and I know that their testimony is true.

Further, we must bear our Cross with its third dimension, which is its height; that is to say, the multitude of sufferings of which it is composed, and which follow one upon another: in this resembling a flood of waters—and Scripture compares them thereto— which we behold gradually increasing, rising and swelling, till at length they overflow.

Finally, we must bear our Cross with its fourth dimension, which is its depth; that is to say, the greatness of the torment which it inflicts, penetrating to the inmost parts, and piercing to the very quick. In all these states we ought never to turn away our eyes from our Divine Master, who, in the fullness of His knowledge, realized at every moment and at once all that He was to suffer successively, in different portions and in different places; who experienced in a marvelous manner all the torments of the martyrs, the persecutions of the faithful, the trials of the Church, the horror of sin, and specially the sins of those to whom His precious death would become useless by their own fault, through their want of correspondence with His love; His abandonment by His Father, by whom He was treated as though He had committed the sins of all mankind. Oh, how strong an affection for the Cross does not this spectacle produce! And, in truth, there are souls whose hungering for it is insatiable, whose thirst cannot he allayed, who are never satiated with opprobrium. But what are we doing, miserable sinners that we are? Alas! We say often enough that we ought to bear the cross, and we do all we can to avoid it, or to get rid of it when we have found it. If it is question of clothing ourselves, we want to have a good coat; of lodging ourselves, a nice house; feeding ourselves, delicate viands; and we neglect nothing that can conduce to our comfort. If we are travelling, we inquire for the best inn, and at the inn for the best chamber, and in the chamber for the best bed. Through all the seasons of the year we are ever on the look-out for fine weather. In short, everywhere and in everything we shall see, if we consider, that we wish to have no cross. If the All-good God sends us one which we cannot avoid, we occupy our imaginations with desiring to be delivered from it; or we fancy that other crosses would be more suitable to us, desiring, with an extreme perversity, to have what we have not, and consequently what God does not require from us; and not to have what we have, .and what God therefore demands from us.

CHAPTER VIII.

THE PERFECT CROSS, AS EXEMPLIFIED IN THE PERSON OF THE SERAPHIC ST. TERESA.

There are crosses which are begun; there are others which are far advanced; and there are some perfect -ones, which are quite finished, which have reached their full completion, and are wanting in nothing. As these last are rare enough, owing to our neglect in utilizing them, our little correspondence with the movements of grace and the designs of God, our lack of vigor and of courage, and, above all, because we do not know how sufficiently to value the gift of God, because we are ungrateful to Him for it, and do not apply ourselves to thank Him, bless Him, love Him for it, suffering with thanksgiving and with the conviction that we are utterly unworthy of it, which is unquestionably true, I have thought of proposing an example of one of the most beautiful crosses, and the most perfect, which our Lord ever planted in His Church, in order to enkindle our frozen hearts, and generously animate us to oppose no obstacle to divine grace, but to abandon ourselves without reserve to all its divine movements, to the end that it may perfectly accomplish the crosses which it is fashioning within us by a special mercy of our Lord Jesus Christ and His most holy Mother.

It is of the divine Teresa I am about to speak, in order that I may just say one single word, in this little treatise, of her most dolorous passion, which, to express myself in the terms of the Apostle (Col. 1:24), is a sacred "filling-up" of the inconceivable "passions," or sufferings, " of our Lord Jesus Christ." The only thing that troubles me is the being obliged, in regard to a subject of such magnitude, to confine myself within the limits which the plan of this little book imposes. Indeed, I may say with truth that the passion, or crosses, of this Christian Amazon would form a high and worthy subject for large and copious volumes: how, then, is it possible to treat it within the space of a short chapter of a work which is itself but a small abridgment? I must therefore frankly avow that what I here present is not so much a portrait of the sufferings of the Saint as a poor slight sketch of them. Only let us adore—you who read this and I together with you—Jesus suffering in the sufferings of St. Teresa; let us honour the Passion of our gracious Saviour in that of His generous servant; let us dwell in thought on the dolors of the Saint, in order to raise ourselves to those of the Saint of Saints. Let us make it sometimes the subject of our meditations and our Communions; let us have the Holy Mass offered in thanksgiving for the grand use which this seraphic soul made of it, to the end that we may obtain by her powerful intercessions the grace to imitate her in her fidelity.

Let us go, then, forthwith, O my soul, to behold this prodigy of grace which has been manifested to the whole Church in our latter days. O God, what a spectacle is presented to our eyes? O my soul, the glimpse that we obtain of it—and, alas! It is but nothing—discovers to us one of the most beautiful and most finished crosses which have ever appeared. I have declared that I would say only one word: in one word, then, I see Heaven, earth, Hell, God, the most holy Virgin, the Angels, the Saints, good people and bad people here below, yea, and the devils themselves, all with one accord combining, albeit with different intentions, to construct this cross. Was ever work fashioned by a greater, a more skilful, or a more experienced multitude of workmen. The matter of which this living cross is composed, includes her body and all its members, her exterior senses, her soul and all its powers; whatever affects her in regard to natural good, temporal or moral, whether you consider what is useful or agreeable, or, again, what is honourable therein; whatever affects her in regard to spiritual and supernatural good: is it possible to imagine a vaster or richer material for crosses? If all sufferings, as this Saint testifies, are so many precious stones, could there be anything more precious or more brilliant than this cross of hers? The strongest eyes of mortal creatures here below must fain close at the sight of so much light; its splendor is too dazzling. But, O my soul, do You not see that this valiant woman, whose price we could hardly match, though we were to search to the farthest regions of the earth,—do You not see that she herself labours to construct her own cross? This it is- that makes it perfect: God wills that in conjunction with all the rest of His creatures, and even with His- own divine hand, we should lay to our own; without this the work is never perfected.

The body of the Saint is nothing but one pure cross. The truth of this we may learn from her own mouth: for she declares that she was full of pains from head to foot. Here is quite enough to crucify anyone, even if the pains were light, by reason of their multitude. But she declares, that they were so poignant that it was thought she was seized with rabies ,A in fact they prevented her taking any rest either by day or even by night, the time to which people look for some relief. She was so dried up and consumed that her sinews were beginning to shrink.

It seemed to her as if her bones were out of joint, and this sometimes to such an extent as to render her insensible; indeed, on one occasion she lay in this state- for the space of four days. She was even believed to- be dead, and was laid out for burial, with tapers burning round her body, her eyes being actually sealed up with the wax which fell upon them. At other times she was like a person who was being strangled, and could not bear that any one should touch her. But perhaps it may be supposed that these bodily torments did not last long? This was not so: for three years she lost the use of her limbs; for twenty years she was afflicted with vomiting.

In the Sixth Chamber of the Interior Castle she says, alluding to herself, that she knew a person who cannot be said to have passed a single day without pain, and that she had all sorts of pains. Observe well these words: "All sorts of pains." Moreover, it must not be supposed that this is a mere imagination! Of one who takes a pleasure in magnifying her sufferings, seeing that, in the judgment of physicians, as recorded in the 32nd chapter of her Life, the pains she endured were the most frightful that can be endured in this world. To sum up all, this incomparable Saint, so truthful in her words, so free from every touch of self-complacency, of a fortitude invincible, the paragon of her sex, declares that God alone knows the torments she suffered in her body: this testimony to the truth she renders in the first chapters of her Life, wherein she relates all that I have here said, although I have not given the reference to the passages themselves. Is it not true, therefore, that her virginal body was a veritable cross, the greatness and the worth of which no man can ever tell, since, as she herself declares, God only knows what were its pains and sufferings?

If the Saint was crucified in body, she was so, in a manner

198

still more perfect, in her soul. The nobility of the soul does not surpass that of the body so much as interior and spiritual crosses surpass those which are corporal and exterior. Led by the Holy Spirit into the interior desert, she spent therein a large proportion of her life, without receiving any of those dews of heaven which do not fail to refresh others, from time to time, in those frightful solitudes. For her they were but as those mountains of Gelboe (2 Kings 1:21) on which no rain ever falls, or as that land of the Psalmist (62:3) where there is no water and no way. She was oppressed with a profound sadness, and knew not what to do with herself amidst all these interior afflictions. From Heaven she received only wounds, while earth tortured her on every side. She was all crucified in her body, she was all crucified in her soul. And if you ask me what these crosses are, the Saint shall herself reply to you, in the history of her life, that God alone knows the sufferings she endured exteriorly, as I have already said; how much more, then, shall her interior sufferings never be known to creatures! Hence, in the Sixth Chamber of the Interior Castle, she declares that such torments have no words to describe them. But if you urge me to give you at least some idea of what she is unable to express —she who was so skilful in describing—she declares in the same place that I have just cited, that these pains were such that she could compare them to nothing save the pains of hell. This is, indeed, to say much about them in few words: and moreover we may form a conjecture as to their intensity, since, after all, she says that they defy description.

But you will say to me, these extraordinary favours which Heaven bestowed upon her, consoled her greatly amidst her sufferings, as also the numerous marks of approbation she received from our gracious Saviour, His holy Mother, and the Angels and the Saints. True it is that this was well capable of comforting her, but amid the horrible pains which she endured, as, for instance, that with which she was seized on the day of establishing her first house, she lost the power of reflecting on the illuminations, the apparitions, and all the other intimations which our Lord vouchsafed her. Besides, the favours she received appeared to be a dream, an imagination; a thousand doubts would occur to her with respect to the greatest of them; she thought she was deceived; and in this view, alas! Her favours, instead of consoling her, were a subject of exceeding distress to her. She thought it might have sufficed to be herself a prey to delusions, without also deluding others.

What, then, will this incomparable Saint do amid all these torments 1 If she seeks relief, God, she says (in the 30th chapter of her Life), does not permit her to find any. Strange cross, whose torments, according to the Saint, are intolerable, and, together with this excess of suffering, leave the soul without succor or relief! If we would enter into ourselves to look for some remedy, we find our eyes bandaged—it is the Saint's own expression; the soul is deprived of the power of thinking a good thought or desiring to make any act of virtue. Faith for the time is as if deadened, as well as all the other virtues. She believes that she has no love of God. It seems as if she had never had any remembrance of Him. The understanding remains at times so obscured that we are as it were without light and without reason; and nothing comes into the mind but what vexes us. If we would apply ourselves to prayer, it is only still more to increase our cross and aggravate our sufferings.

The Saint tried to do exterior good works, and she says that this availed her little. If she retired into solitude, it was only to find torture; if she conversed with any one, she suffered much; for conversation at such times is unendurable; one feels oneself in a temper to eat everybody up. If she gave herself to reading, she derived no profit from it. Often, when she spoke of her state to her confessors, they rated and harshly rebuked her, whatever resolutions they might have made to the contrary; and on several occasions all the assurance they gave her had no effect in consoling her, although she implicitly obeyed their directions: it seemed to her that she was unable to explain herself, that she never made herself understood, or that she was deceiving them. True, God at least remained to her, but she thought she was rejected by Him; she regarded Him as adverse and opposed to her, and believed that she no longer had access to the presence of His Divine Majesty. At the time of the great festivals her torments were redoubled. She was deprived of all consolation, both from Heaven and from earth. She was as insensible to good as a beast. She was crucified in body, in mind, in her whole self; by her thoughts, her memory, her imagination; by prayer, by virtues, by good works, by reading, by solitude, by conversation, by all creatures: created things were to her as to the damned, so far as regarded suffering. In fine, she was crucified by God Himself. All this is drawn out in detail in the 30th chapter of her Life, and in the Sixth Chamber of the Interior Castle, although she speaks of it also in several other places..

In addition to all this, it must be observed that the contradictions of men served greatly to fashion and adorn a cross so precious. She saw herself brought into collision with almost all sorts of persons, of all states and conditions. The nobles took part against her, the magistrates were strongly opposed to her, the royal officers, the governor of the town in which she established her first monastery, exerted all their authority strenuously against her. In several public meetings, at which all the corporate bodies were convened, resolutions were passed having for their object the destruction of her holiest designs. And what was specially alarming, the populace, who are usually guided only by their caprices and are apt to be carried away into all sorts of excesses, became highly excited against the Saint, inveighed loudly against her, hurled abusive language at her, and declared they would pull down her poor house by main force, the governor himself threatening to break in the door and drive out four destitute orphan girls who were the first and truly worthy subjects of the Carmelite reform. But this is not all: this would have been little if she had not suffered also from ecclesiastics, religious, prelates, her own sisters, her superiors, her general, her friends, her confessors, and those who in other respects endeavoured to stand by her.

She suffered from the princes of this world, say the lessons 1 read on her feast day; but she also suffered much from the princes and prelates of the Church. With all modesty, but with perfect frankness, she wrote, in reference to one of these prelates, that it seemed as if God had raised him up in order to try her patience. Her General, who had told her she might found as many houses as she had hairs on her head, became wholly changed, imprisoned her in her own convent, and prohibited her from undertaking anything whatever, thus rendering her to all appearance useless. The nuns of the monastery where she was when she first proposed establishing her reform, indignantly complained that she insulted them, and talked of putting her in confinement. Her confessors, as has been said, reproved her in a most distressing manner, disapproved her conduct, and found fault with her slow progress, as they accounted it, telling her that the favours she received were illusions, and that she was deceived by the devil;

and, while they were writing most offensive letters to her, they were themselves receiving warnings to be on their guard against her. The affair, in short, arrived at such a point that she could do nothing but weep, being afraid that she would not find a confessor willing to receive her confession. " Alas," she cries, " if I thought sometimes to receive consolation from a confessor, it seemed as if all the devils in hell were in league to persuade him to torment me." But more than this: she suffered even with reference to those of her directors who stood boldly forward in her defense, as, for instance, that saintly man, Father Baltasar Alvarez; and for this reason, that she was extremely pained on learning the persecutions they were undergoing on her account. Their conduct was excessively blamed, at the same time that her own was condemned. I may here add that her friends contributed not a little to her crucifixion. Some interpreted her actions in a manner unfavorable to her; others believed she was wanting in humility - some took exception to her conduct, while others accused her of obstinacy, because she did not follow their advice.

In the history of the Order it is related how her friends met together, and came to the resolution of having her exorcised, like one possessed. Sometimes they were fairly bewildered with the numerous counsels they received as to standing on their guard against her and being very cautious in their own behavior with regard to her. It was indeed a great trouble to the Saint to have to encounter all these opponents on the occasion of founding her first monastery. After much time had been consumed in disputes and noisy clamor, in transactions and processes on the subject of this establishment, the governor and the town promised to offer no further opposition, and declared they would be satisfied, provided the monastery were endowed. Her friends, after deliberating on the subject, considered that it was necessary to content the governor and the town; that it was unadvisable to continue the contest, and thus even to endanger a foundation of such importance for a matter not absolutely incompatible with that perfection of observance which it was designed to establish. History affirms that all her friends were of this opinion. However, to give it more weight, they proposed consulting doctors; and the judgment of the doctors coincided with that of all her friends. Only conceive the extremity to which, under these circumstances, this great Saint was reduced: she could not resolve to accept an endowment, but in this her opinion was diametrically opposed to that of the doctors and her friends; and, as she remained firm in her sentiments, she had to pass for an -obstinate -woman, who acted according to her own ideas, and would not submit herself, and allow it to be believed that she was under a delusion and had no real .and solid virtue. True, she acted on the advice of that holy man, Father Peter of Alcantara, who had instructed her that in a matter which concerned perfection doctors were not the persons to be consulted, and that it was necessary to have practical experience of poverty in order to speak worthily of it. This agrees with what the Saint herself has written— that on matters of faith, and to know whether actions are conformable to reason, it is necessary to consult doctors, and that she had never been misled by them; but that, in respect to other matters, they ought not to interfere in what they do not understand. I have given the Saint's testimony at length in my book of The Reign of God in Mental Prayer, in the chapters in which I have treated of directors and direction. This seraphic soul, then, did not act by her own lights, but this availed little in her defense, as the doctors and her friends held a different opinion from that of the Blessed Peter of Alcantara.

Behold, then, the terrible situation in which our Saint is placed—opposed by all sorts of persons and, what is most distressing, persecuted by the good as well as by the bad. Let us consider a little what it is she suffers from these contradictions. If slander be one of the greatest persecutions, it must be confessed that hers was very great; since not only did people speak evil of her, but they said all sorts of evil of her. Here is what the pious Bishop of Tarazona wrote in his Life of her:—The evil things that were deposed against the holy mother and the monks and nuns of her Order, and the charges that were brought against them, were so numerous that we may say there was no disgraceful act with which any low, worthless woman might be reproached which was not alleged to blacken and injuriously asperse the character of the Saint; since, even as regarded purity of life, infamous epithets were applied to her, such as might be used respecting a courtesan, a woman destitute of the fear of God. God even permitted that, in one of her journeys, she should be ill-treated by a woman who, under the belief that she had robbed her of one of her clogs, struck her with the other a number of blows upon her head, causing her grievous pains, and at the same time assailing her with a volley of abuse. In order to give publicity to these slanders, several defamatory papers and pamphlets were circulated, and an attempt was made to establish a general agreement out of all these lies. By this means her reputation was ruinously damaged, not only in the privacy of men's houses, but in places of public resort; nay, even in cloisters, and before her very face: on every side she was the object of unceasing attacks. In a public assembly held in the town of Medina, a religious who enjoyed a high reputation spoke very ill of her, and represented her as a creature filled with the spirit of lying, who had made herself notorious throughout Spain. On founding her house at Toledo, the women of the neighborhood assailed her most offensively with their tongues, and would sometimes come to the very convent grate for the purpose of insulting her outrageously.

What will this incomparable Saint do in the midst of all these tempests? If she expresses herself freely, people cry out at her arrogance; they declare her virtue to be imaginary, because she lacks humility. If she replies, when questioned as to her interior state, they say she wants to make a display of spirituality, and to set herself up as a teacher. Should she say anything inadvertently and without much attention, these servants of God would twist it from its purpose and discover all sorts of latent consequences. It would be impossible to describe the lecturing, the ridicule, the reprimands for her extravagances which she had to endure. When she first proposed her reform, the nuns of the house where she was exclaimed that she was doing them a wrong, and ought to be put in prison. But the strangest trial of all was that which she endured at the hands of her General. As he was a very holy man, it was not possible to suspect him of not having the best intentions; as he had large experience and was possessed of great wisdom, it would have been useless to say that he was not acting with sufficient prudence; as he entertained a high regard for her, it was easy to be convinced that he had no wish to oppose her; as he had shown such confidence in her as to make use of her services, it was judged that he must have good reasons for altering his conduct towards her; as he had caused many inquiries to be instituted respecting her, formal replies to which had been given him at a General Chapter of the Carmelites of the mitigated rule, and as he had taken the advice of the sagest Fathers there assembled and everything had been done according to rule, it could not be supposed that either prejudice or deception had had any share in the business. Besides, there were witnesses and deponents, who accused her of very grievous offences. Posterity knows well that the testimonies were false, but the falsehood was not then detected. In course of time it became manifest that this General had in fact allowed himself to be influenced by prejudice, and had been imposed upon; that, holy man as he was, he had inflicted suffering of a most distressing kind on one who was the great prodigy of grace in his day; but at the time these things were hidden and unknown. What is also most remarkable is that almost all the Fathers of the mitigated rule were opposed to the Saint. Now, how could it reasonably be expected that more account should be taken of the sentiments of one woman, backed by a small number of persons, than of nearly all the religious of an Order? Add to this, that it seemed that in the interests of peace she ought at least to have desisted, since there was no other way of allaying the disturbance. And further, as has been said, the opposition she encountered proceeded, not only from ill intentioned persons, carried away by passion or by envy, but from those whose authority was so high that not to defer to their judgment was grievously to offend them. It seemed to be a disparagement to their virtues, their lights, and their qualities generally. Thus it was that, in addition to the formal processes before her Order, information were also taken against the Saint on the part of the Inquisition, on account of the exalted position of the persons who accused her, and the high estimation in which they were regarded; and the prosecution was so far advanced that every day it was expected she would have to be committed to prison together with her nuns.

However, as it was not possible to suppress the splendor of her virtues, and even the extraordinary favours she had received were known to many, it was objected that these favours were illusions of the devil, or, at least, were the offspring of her imagination; that her virtues were only apparent, and that in reality she was a proud person and a hypocrite, as, indeed, some took the trouble of coming and telling her to her face; that she rushed into extremes; that she was an impostor, and precautions ought to be taken against her; that she was a gadabout, hare-brained creature, and would have done much better to remain quiet in her convent, living there as a good religious, and performing the ordinary exercises of the community like the rest.

O my God, how far removed are Your ways from the ways of men! O worldly wisdom, O human prudence, what becomes of you here? So it is: the Spirit of my God is ever the same; all His greatest designs are accomplished only by the greatest crosses. Never look for great effects of grace where you do not see extraordinary oppositions. Projects which all the world applauds, which procure only honour and approbation to those who undertake them, mark no great operations of the Spirit of God. Rest assured that Hell will ever be on the alert if there be anything which it greatly dreads. Believe me, the world will always be the world, that is to say, always the enemy of those who are truly opposed to it, caring only for God Alone. Ah, well, Teresa is destined to found a great number of religious houses. Human prudence says that this cannot be done without much money; but she has not a penny, she is reduced to an extremity of poverty truly alarming. This prudence says that she has need of an unassailed reputation, especially as she undertakes to reform, not women only, but men; and yet her honour is compromised on all sides, she is the laughing-stock of society. This prudence considers that at least she ought to be strongly supported, in order to protect her against these indignities, and allow free scope for the execution of her plans; whereas everywhere she meets with nothing but contradictions, on the part of prelates, superiors, the monks and nuns of her own Order, her friends, those among the great ones of this world who have sided against her, in short, on the part of persons of all kinds: and they who were the most opposed to her were those who enjoyed the greatest popularity. The prelate Sega persisted obstinately in the belief that the reform ought to be prevented; condemning, imprisoning, and banishing with the greatest rigor those who he thought were able to resist him; commanding, under pain of divers censures, all who were laboring in its cause to dismiss it from their thoughts and take no further part in the matter. They who persuaded the Father General to lay a strict injunction on the Saint to abandon the undertaking imagined they were thereby rendering that reform impossible, and consigning the glorious reformer to a state of utter despondency.

But how many deceive themselves in the measures they take! He who dwells in the Heavens laughs to scorn all their efforts, which are as naught before His Most Adorable Majesty. In His Divine Presence all their wisdom shrinks into nothing. He takes delight in shattering to pieces all the means they employ to combat His designs, only in order to establish them the more strongly. This is the way in which the Almighty triumphs over the wisest of this world, conducting all things to their ends by means which, according to human prudence, are calculated only to destroy them. Yes, O my Lord and my God, Your greatest works are wrought in nothingness; Your grandest structures are erected only on awful ruins. The living stones that compose them are those whom the world casts out upon the dunghill, and judges to be useless and of no value. Every age has signally displayed this wise and powerful procedure on the part of God, but men are very slow in opening their eyes; they discern it in the ages that have gone before, and they are totally blind to it in the times in which they live. All the faithful now see clearly that every persecution which St. Teresa underwent, and which threatened herself and her Order with total destruction, served only to establish it more gloriously; but this was a thing that was hidden from most persons of her time. Assuredly it must be confessed that our lights are very limited. "Who would have ever thought that his brethren's envy would have proved the great promoter of all Joseph's glory 1 Could a policy which sought to ruin a man have taken surer measures to effect its purpose, than those which were employed by his brothers? Who would not have said of the hapless Joseph, 'Behold a man irretrievably ruined? But, O Providence of my God, how wonderful You are! His very ruin brings about his glorious elevation. They who labour to destroy him, are those who unwittingly are laboring to make him one of the greatest men on earth. Oh, who is like unto our God, who from the height of His heavenly throne regards with complacency those who are in the most abject states of life, that He may raise them from the dust and set them among the princes of His people! I would ask—if all Joseph's brethren had conspired together with one accord, neglecting no means and using all their endeavors to make their brother's fortune, what would they have done, what could they have done? But striving, in their envy, to destroy him, they became, in the hands of Divine Providence, the instruments for raising him to be a viceroy, and one of the most famous men the world has ever seen. This is what this great Patriarch himself truly remarks, when, speaking to his brethren, who were struck with exceeding great fear after they had recognized him, he told them (Gen. 45:8) that it was not so much by their counsel as by the will of God he had been sent into Egypt.

But let us return to our saint, and, having seen her all crucified in body and mind, both by the hand of God and by that of men, let us behold her also fastened to the cross by the devils themselves: she must needs suffer in everything and from everything. Thus the All good God made her suffer for the sins of others, enduring the pains which they deserved, that she might obtain for them the grace which the Divine Mercy accorded to them. The devils not only made her suffer by their stratagems, speaking to her interior words and appearing to her under the form of our Lord in order to deceive her, but tormented her frightfully by their fury, and this with such frequency that she declares that, were she to attempt to relate it all, she would tire out all her hearers. These wretched spirits sometimes tried to stifle her, and swooped down upon her in legions, inflicting on her the most cruel sufferings.

Her generous soul, amid all these torments, went on right royally, like a queen in her own realm and in truth, Jesus having entered into glory by these means, it is by these same ways that the saints are made partakers of it, and reign eternally with Him in His kingdom, which shall have no end.

Come, O my Lord Jesus, come; let Your kingdom come, Your name be hallowed, and Your Divine will be done on earth as it is in Heaven. Amen. Amen.

CROWNING PERFECTION OF GOD'S WORKS.

O admirable Virgin Mother, most justly does the Church
sing that Your abode is in the plenitude of the Saints, seeing
that the All good God has made of Your sacred person a
complete epitome, as it were, of all the graces which He
has bestowed on His elect! You are the great masterpiece
of the Almighty in all the ways of perfection, and, by
consequence, in the holy ways of the Cross among the rest.
Meet, then, it is that I should finish this work at Your feet,
where also I began it, placing it unreservedly in Your sacred
hands, that You may give it the perfection which Your
beloved Son would wish it to have, for the sole glory and
in the sole interest of God Alone, the Most Holy Trinity,
Father, Son, and Holy Ghost. Amen. Amen. Amen.

The End.

OTHER TITLES OFFERED BY

Church Ornaments of Our Own Manufacture

The Spiritual Conflict and Conquest
by Dom Juan Castiniza, O.S.B.

St Alphonsus Liguori on the Council of Trent

Dignity and Duties of the Priest or Selva
by St Alphonsus Liguori

The Maxims and Sayings of St Philip Neri

The Triumph of the Cross
by Savonarola

Indifferentism
or Is One Religion as Good as Another?

Explanation of the Psalms and Canticles
in the Divine Office
by St Alphonsus Liguori

Collection of Catholic Prayers and Devotions
based on the 1957 Raccolta